ALFRED'S
BASIC ADULT
PIANO
COURSE

LESSON BOOK   LEVEL ONE

Jaanvi

P9-CEX-348

WILLARD A. PALMER   MORTON MANUS   AMANDA VICK LETHCO

Correlated materials to be used with Adult Lesson Book, Level 1:

A CD 💿 (14039) and a General Midi disk 💾 (8490) are available, each including a full piano recording and background accompaniment.

Alfred's Basic Adult Piano Course is designed for the adult beginner who wishes to learn the piano by playing chords quickly. The course has a number of features that make it particularly successful in achieving this goal. It progresses very smoothly, with no gaps that cause the skipping of hard sections. In addition, it teaches chords for both hands. Because of this, the pieces in Alfred's Basic are more musical and make playing a richer, more rewarding experience.

Also taught is the understanding of how chords are formed. Instead of memorizing chords, students learn how to derive them regardless of what key they are playing in. Finally, the choice of song material is outstanding, with some popular and familiar favorites mixed with tuneful originals, all adding to the fun and enjoyment of making music.

The student is encouraged to use the compact disc recording or the General MIDI disk. Playing along with these recordings is not only enjoyable, but is invaluable for reinforcing musical concepts such as rhythm, dynamics and phrasing.

2

Contents

How to Sit at the Piano

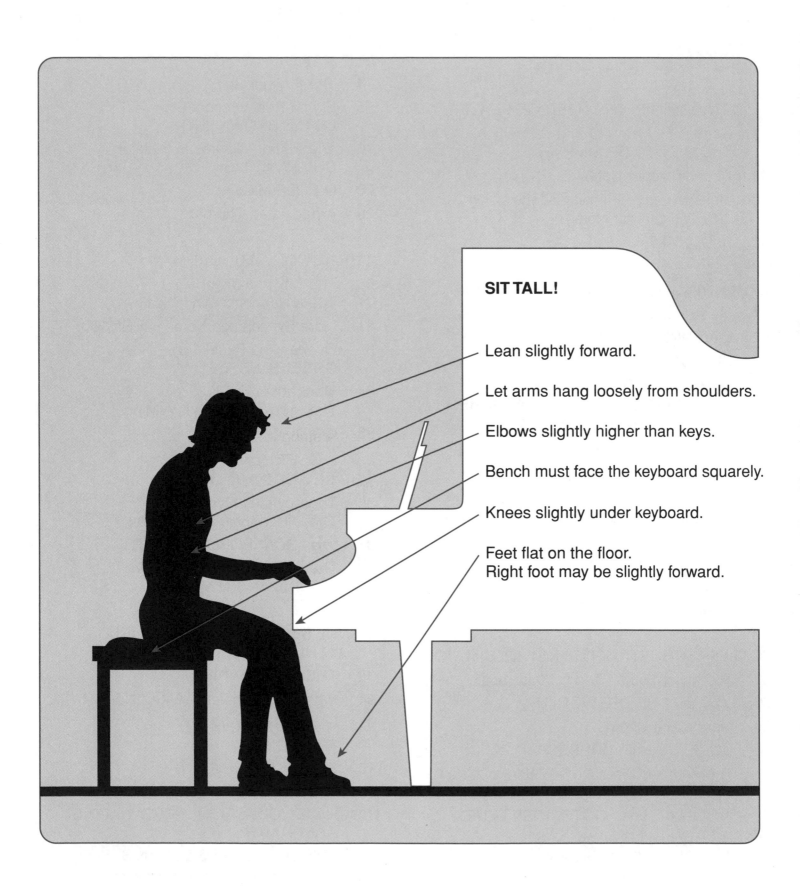

SIT TALL!

Lean slightly forward.

Let arms hang loosely from shoulders.

Elbows slightly higher than keys.

Bench must face the keyboard squarely.

Knees slightly under keyboard.

Feet flat on the floor.
Right foot may be slightly forward.

Finger Numbers

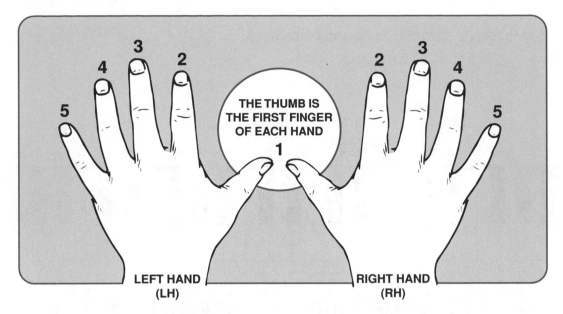

THE THUMB IS
THE FIRST FINGER
OF EACH HAND
1

LEFT HAND
(LH)

RIGHT HAND
(RH)

Response to reading finger numbers should be automatic. Before you begin to play, practice moving each finger as you say its number aloud.

Piano Tones

When you play a key, a hammer inside your piano touches a string to make a tone.
When you drop into a key with a LITTLE weight, you make a SOFT tone.
When you use MORE weight, you make a LOUDER tone.

String

Hammer

Curve your fingers when you play!

Pretend you have a bubble in your hand.

Hold the bubble gently, so it doesn't break!

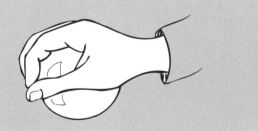

1. Play any white key with the 3rd finger of either hand, softly.
2. See how many times you can repeat the same key, making each tone a little louder.

Before you play any key, you should always decide how soft or loud you want it to sound.

For the first pieces in this book, play with a MODERATELY LOUD tone.

The Keyboard

The keyboard is made up of white keys and black keys.
The black keys are in groups of twos and threes.

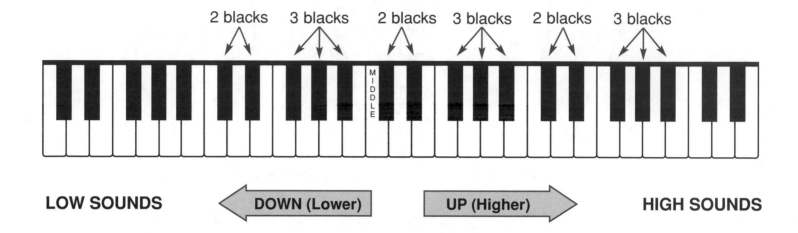

2 blacks   3 blacks   2 blacks   3 blacks   2 blacks   3 blacks

LOW SOUNDS   DOWN (Lower)   UP (Higher)   HIGH SOUNDS

On the keyboard, DOWN is to the LEFT, and UP is to the RIGHT.
As you move LEFT, the tones sound LOWER. As you move RIGHT, the tones sound HIGHER.

Play the 2-BLACK-KEY groups!

LH

1. Using LH 2 3, begin at the middle and play all the 2-black-key groups going **DOWN** the keyboard (both keys at once).

2. Using RH 2 3, begin at the middle and play all the 2-black-key groups going **UP** the keyboard (both keys at once).

RH

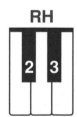

Play the 3-BLACK-KEY groups!

LH

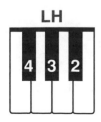

3. Using LH 2 3 4, begin at the middle and play all the 3-black-key groups going **DOWN** the keyboard (all three keys at once).

4. Using RH 2 3 4, begin at the middle and play all the 3-black-key groups going **UP** the keyboard (all three keys at once).

RH

Name That Key!

Piano keys are named for the first seven letters of the alphabet, beginning with **A**.

A B C D E F G

Each white key is recognized by its position in or next to a black-key group!
For example: **A**'s are found between the **TOP TWO KEYS** of each **3-BLACK-KEY GROUP.**

Play the following. Use LH 3 for keys below the middle of the keyboard.
Use RH 3 for keys above the middle of the keyboard.
Say the name of each key aloud as you play!

Play all the **A**'s
on your piano.

Play all the **B**'s.

Play all the **C**'s.

Play all the **D**'s.

Play all the **E**'s.

Play all the **F**'s.

Play all the **G**'s.

You can now name every white key on your piano!
The key names are **A B C D E F G**, used over and over!

The lowest key
on your piano
is **A**.

The C nearest the
middle of the piano is
called **MIDDLE C.**

The highest key
on your piano
is **C**.

Going **UP** the keyboard, the notes sound **HIGHER and HIGHER!**

Play and name every white key beginning with bottom A.
Use LH 3 for keys below middle C, and RH 3 for keys above middle C.

You are now ready to begin ADULT THEORY BOOK 1 and ADULT FLASHCARDS.

Right Hand C Position

Place the RH on the keyboard so that the **1st FINGER** falls on **MIDDLE C**.
Let the remaining 4 fingers fall naturally on the next 4 white keys.
Keep the fingers curved and relaxed.

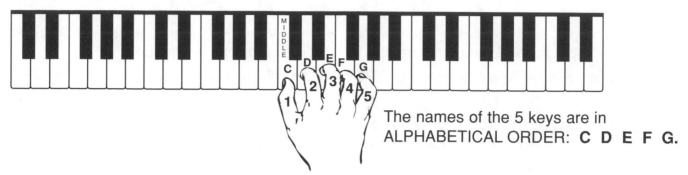

The names of the 5 keys are in
ALPHABETICAL ORDER: **C D E F G.**

Notes for this position are written on the TREBLE STAFF.

The TREBLE STAFF has 5 lines and 4 spaces.

Middle C is written on a short line below the staff, called a *leger* line.

D is written in the space below the staff.

Each next higher note is written on the next higher line or space.

TREBLE CLEF SIGN: used for RH notes.

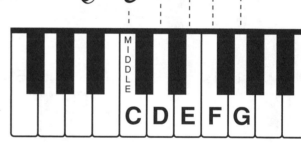

RIGHT HAND WARM-UP 🔊 *

Play the following *WARM-UP.* Say the name of each note aloud as you play.
Repeat until you can play smoothly and evenly. As the notes go higher on the keyboard,
they are written higher on the staff!

* 🔊 This symbol indicates the track number of the selection on the CD. See the General MIDI (GM) disk
sleeve for the GM track numbers.

Quarter Notes & Half Notes

Music is made up of **short** tones and **long** tones. We write these tones in **notes,** and we measure their lengths by **counting**. The combining of notes into patterns is called RHYTHM.

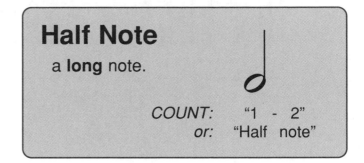

Clap (or tap) the following rhythm. Clap ONCE for each note, counting aloud.
Notice how the BAR LINES divide the music into MEASURES of equal duration.

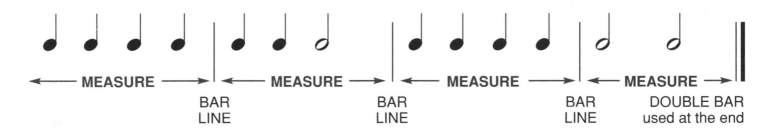

ODE TO JOY *(Theme from Beethoven's 9th Symphony)*

1. Clap (or tap) the rhythm evenly, counting aloud.
2. Play & sing (or say) the finger numbers.
3. Play & count.
4. Play & sing (or say) the note names.

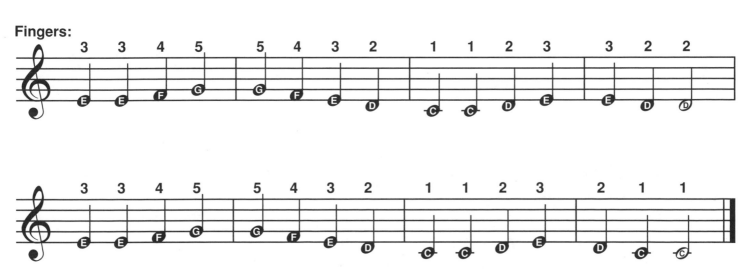

You are now ready to begin ADULT SIGHT READING BOOK 1.

Left Hand C Position

Place the LH on the keyboard so that the **5th FINGER** falls on the **C BELOW** (to the left of) **MIDDLE C.**
Let the remaining fingers fall naturally on the next 4 white keys.
Keep the fingers curved and relaxed.

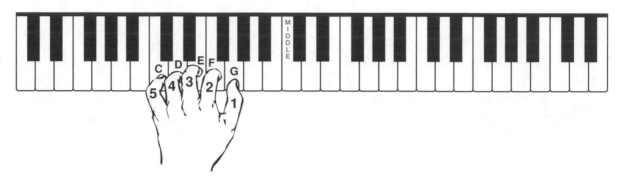

Notes for this position are written on the BASS STAFF.

The BASS STAFF also has 5 lines and 4 spaces.

The C, played by 5, is written on the second space of the staff.

Each next higher note is written on the next higher line or space.

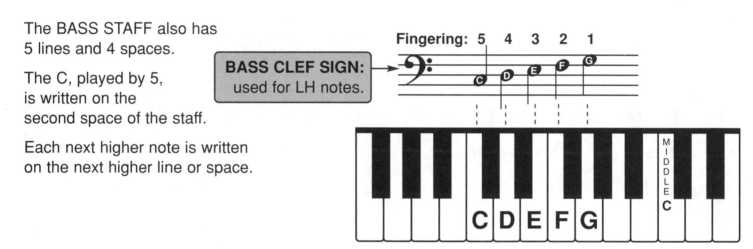

LEFT HAND WARM-UP

Play the following *WARM-UP.* Say the name of each note aloud as you play.
Repeat until you can play smoothly and evenly.

When notes are BELOW the MIDDLE LINE of the staff, the stems usually point UP.
When notes are ON or ABOVE the MIDDLE LINE, the stems usually point DOWN.

The Whole Note

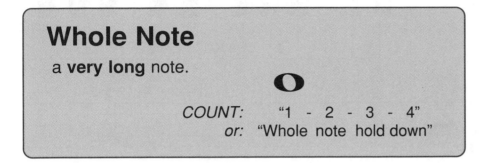

Whole Note

a **very long** note.

COUNT: "1 - 2 - 3 - 4"
or: "Whole note hold down"

Clap (or tap) the following rhythm. Clap ONCE for each note, counting aloud.

AURA LEE 🔊⁵

This melody was made into a popular song, *"LOVE ME TENDER,"* sung by Elvis Presley.

1. Clap (or tap) the rhythm, counting aloud.
2. Play & sing (or say) the finger numbers.
3. Play & count.
4. Play & sing (or say) the note names.

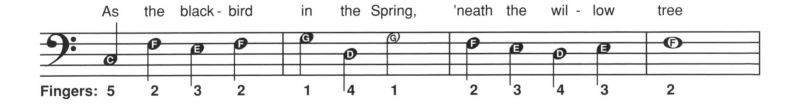

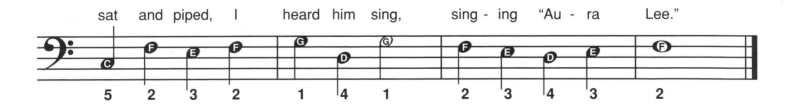

The Grand Staff

The BASS STAFF and TREBLE STAFF, when joined together with a BRACE, make up the **GRAND STAFF.**

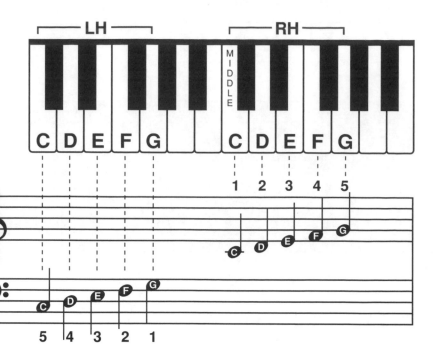

Treble Clef →

Brace →

Bass Clef →

TIME SIGNATURE

Music has numbers at the beginning called the **TIME SIGNATURE.**

4/4 means **4** beats to each measure.

means a **QUARTER NOTE** ♩ gets one beat.

PLAYING ON THE GRAND STAFF

Only the starting finger number for each hand is given.

The following practice procedure is recommended for the rest of the pieces in this book:

1. Clap (or tap) & count.
2. Play & count.
3. Play & sing the words, if any.

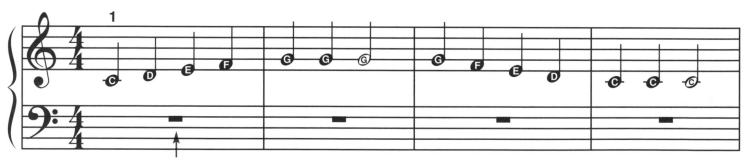

This sign ▬ is a **WHOLE REST.**
LH is silent a whole measure!

RH silent a whole measure.

The double dots mean *repeat from the beginning.*

You are now ready to begin ADULT FINGER AEROBICS.

ROCK-ALONG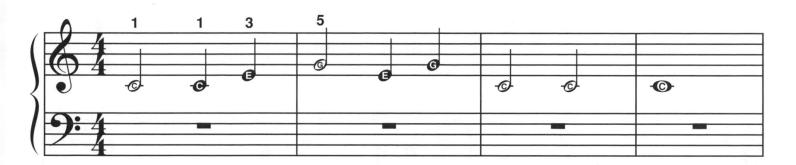

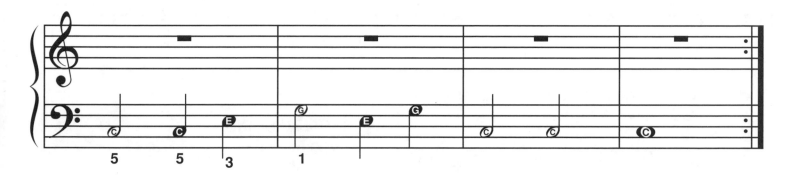

MEXICAN HAT DANCE

This sign 𝄽 is a QUARTER REST.
Rest for one count!

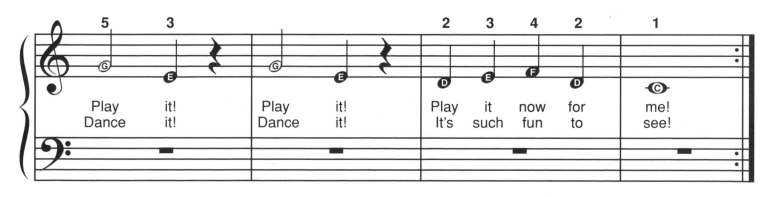

You are now ready to begin ADULT DUET BOOK 1.

Melodic Intervals

Distances between tones are measured in **INTERVALS,** called 2nds, 3rds, 4ths, 5ths, etc.

Notes played *separately* make a *melody.*

We call the intervals between these notes **MELODIC INTERVALS.**

Play these MELODIC 2nds & 3rds. Listen to the sound of each interval.

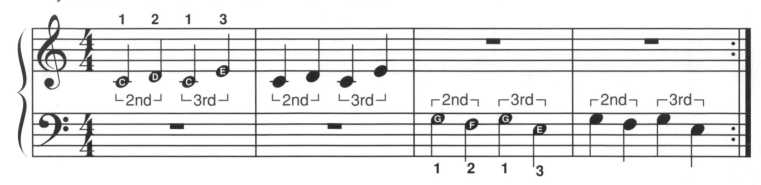

The following excerpts contain only repeated notes and MELODIC 2nds & 3rds.

AU CLAIRE DE LA LUNE

> **DYNAMIC SIGNS**
> tell how loud or
> soft to play.
>
> *p* (piano) = soft

TISKET, A TASKET

> *mf* (mezzo forte) = moderately loud

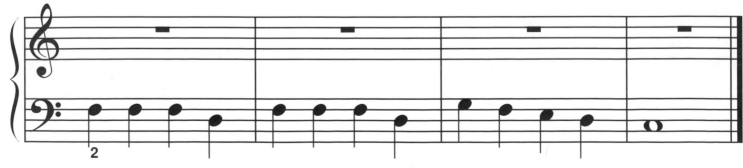

Harmonic Intervals

Notes played *together* make *harmony*.
We call the intervals between these notes **HARMONIC INTERVALS.**

Play these HARMONIC 2nds & 3rds. Listen to the sound of each interval.

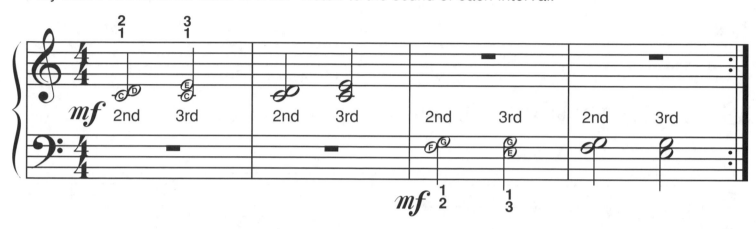

ROCKIN' INTERVALS

$\boldsymbol{f}$ *(forte)* = loud

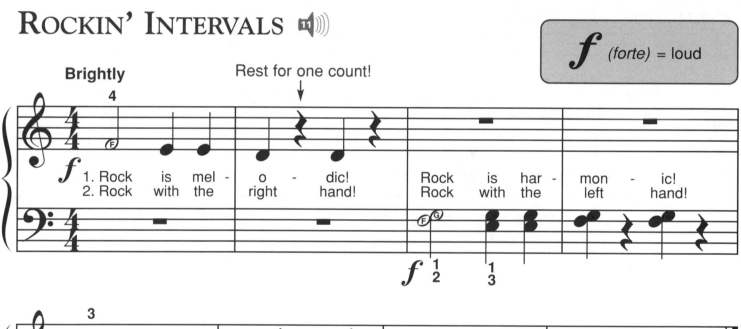

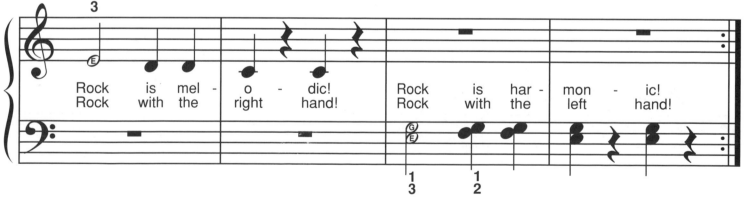

DUET PART: (Student plays 1 octave higher.)

Melodic 4ths & 5ths

Play these MELODIC 4ths & 5ths.
Listen to the sound of each interval.

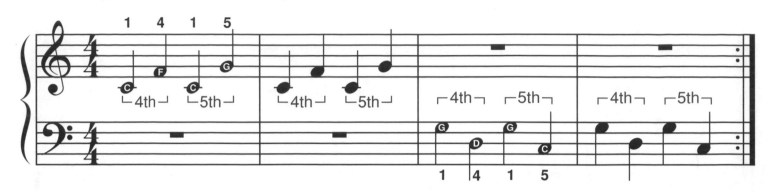

GOOD KING WENCESLAS 🔊 Find the 4ths before you play!

Moderately fast

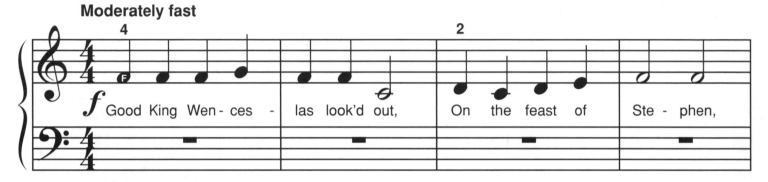

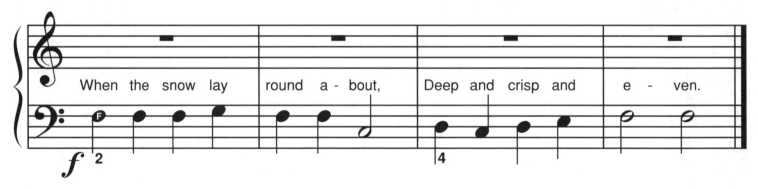

MY FIFTH 🔊 Find the 5ths before you play!

Seriously

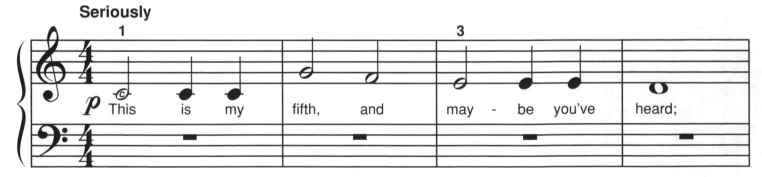

Harmonic 4ths & 5ths

Play these HARMONIC 4ths & 5ths.
Listen to the sound of each interval.

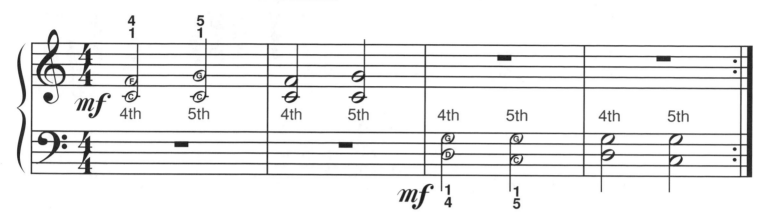

JINGLE BELLS

Before you play: 1. Find all the MELODIC 4ths & 5ths in the RH.
2. Find all the HARMONIC 4ths & 5ths in the LH.

Merrily

Jin - gle, bells! Jin - gle, bells! Jin - gle all the way!

Oh, what fun it is to ride a one-horse o - pen sleigh!

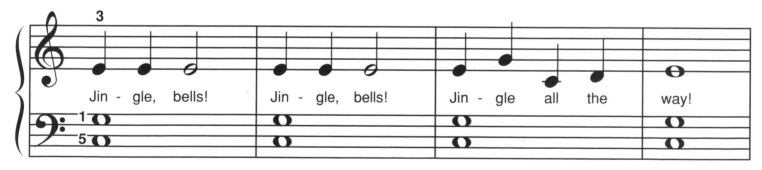

Jin - gle, bells! Jin - gle, bells! Jin - gle all the way!

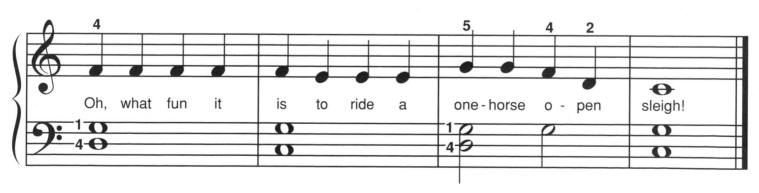

Oh, what fun it is to ride a one-horse o - pen sleigh!

The C Major Chord

A chord is three or more notes played together.
The **C MAJOR CHORD** is made of three notes: **C E G.**

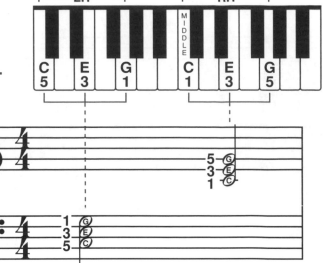

Be sure to play all three chord notes
exactly together, with fingers nicely curved.

C MAJOR CHORDS for LH

Play & count.

C MAJOR CHORDS for RH

Play & count.

C MAJOR CHORDS for BOTH HANDS

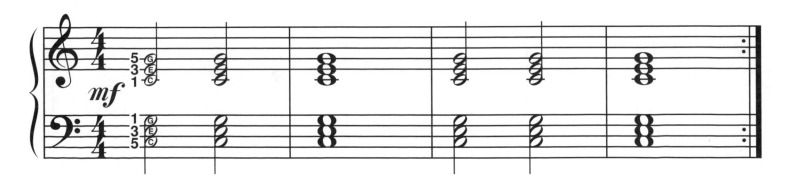

Brother John

Read by patterns! For RH, think:
"C, up a 2nd, up a 2nd, down a 3rd," etc.
Think the pattern, then *play* it!

Moderately fast

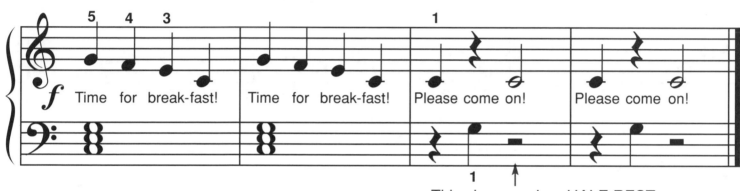

This sign ▬ is a HALF REST.
Rest for two counts!

Here's a Happy Song!

Read by patterns! For LH, think:
"G, down a 2nd, down a 2nd," etc.

Happily

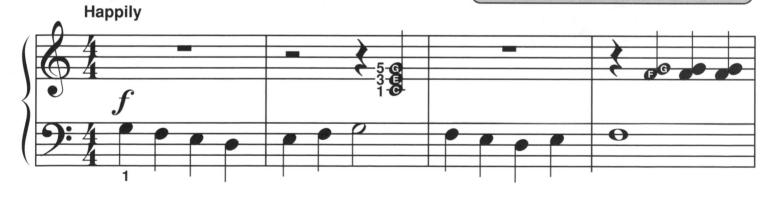

Introducing Ⓑ for Left Hand

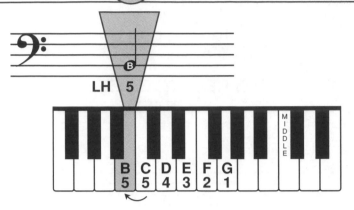

LH 5

TO FIND B:

Place the LH in **C POSITION**.
Reach finger 5 one white key to the left!

Play slowly. Say the note names as you play.

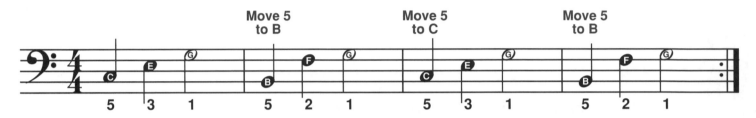

Two Important Chords

Two frequently used chords are **C MAJOR** & **G⁷**.

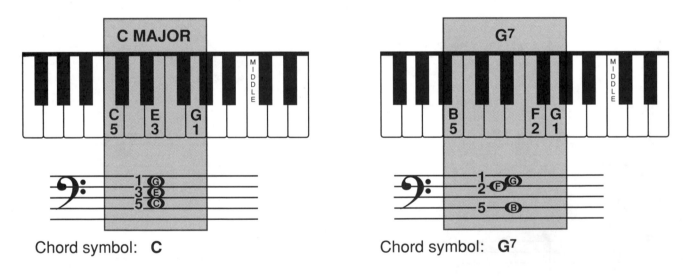

Chord symbol: **C**

Chord symbol: **G⁷**

Chord symbols are always used in popular music to identify chord names.

Practice changing from the C chord to the G⁷ chord and back again:
1. The 1st finger plays G in both chords.
2. The 2nd finger plays F in the G⁷ chord.
3. Only the 5th finger moves out of C POSITION (down to B) for G⁷.

TIED NOTES: When notes on the *same* line or space are joined with a curved line, we call them *tied notes.*

The key is held down for the
COMBINED VALUES OF BOTH NOTES!

Count: "1 - 2 - 3 - 4,   1 - 2 - 3 - 4."

MERRILY WE ROLL ALONG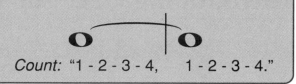

Play the RH & LH separately at first, then together. Practice the RH *mf* and the LH *p*.
The melody should always be clearly heard above the accompaniment.

LARGO *(from "The New World")* 🔊

This melody is also known as *GOING HOME.*

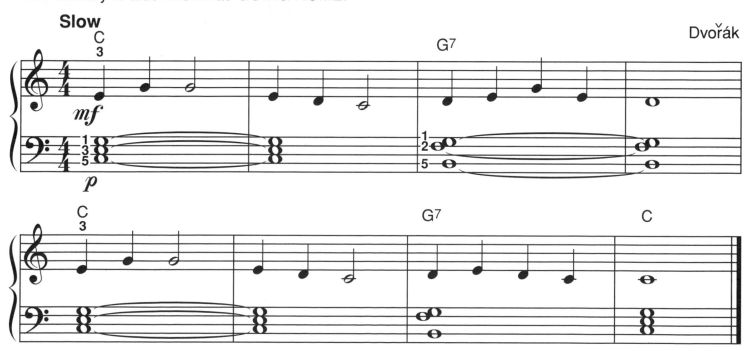

*In most popular sheet music, the chord symbols appear ABOVE the RH melody.
 The symbol appears ONLY WHEN THE CHORD CHANGES.

Introducing B for Right Hand

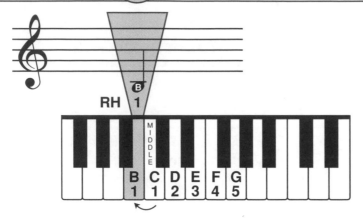

RH 1

TO FIND B:

Place the RH in **C POSITION.**

Reach finger 1 one white key to the left!

Play slowly. Say the note names as you play.

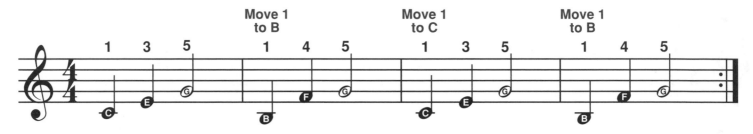

C & G⁷ Chords for Right Hand

It is very important to be able to play all chords with the RIGHT hand as well as the LEFT.
Chords are used in either or both hands in popular and classical music.

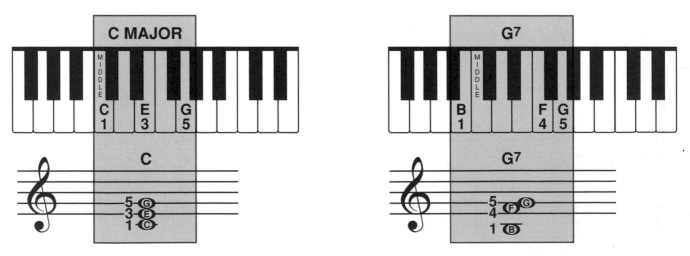

Practice changing from the C chord to the G⁷ chord and back again:
1. The 5th finger plays G in both chords.
2. The 4th finger plays F in the G⁷ chord.
3. Only the 1st finger moves out of C POSITION (down to B) for G⁷.

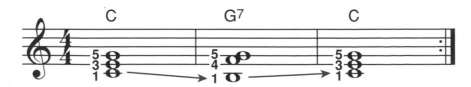

MARY ANN

Calypso tune

All day, all night, Ma - ry Ann, (Ma - ry Ann,)

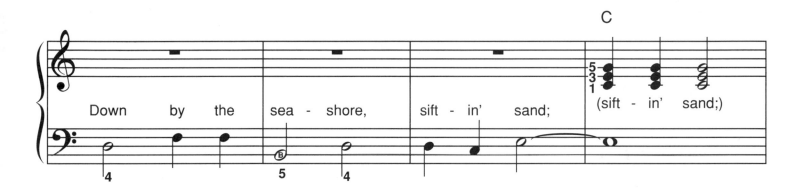

Down by the sea - shore, sift - in' sand; (sift - in' sand;)

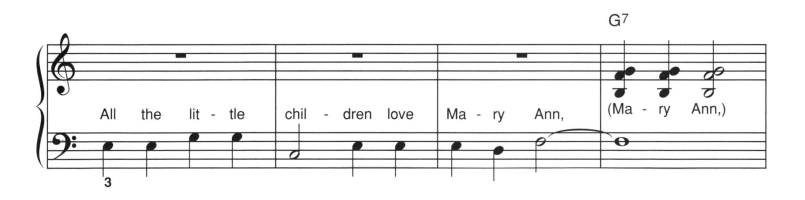

All the lit - tle chil - dren love Ma - ry Ann, (Ma - ry Ann,)

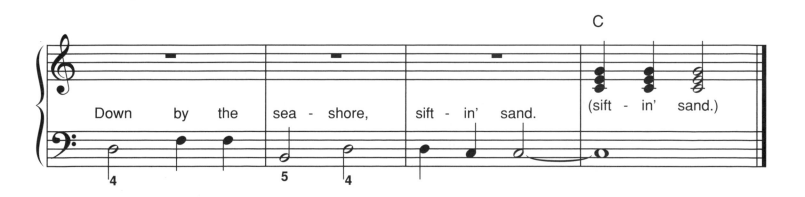

Down by the sea - shore, sift - in' sand. (sift - in' sand.)

New Time Signature

Dotted Half Note

3/4 means **3** beats to each measure.

3/4 means a **QUARTER NOTE** ♩ gets one beat.

A **DOTTED HALF NOTE** gets 3 counts.
(2 counts for the half note,
plus 1 count for the dot!) 𝅗𝅥·

COUNT: "1 - 2 - 3"

Clap (or tap) the following rhythm.
Clap **ONCE** for each note, counting aloud.

ROCKETS 🔊

Moderately fast

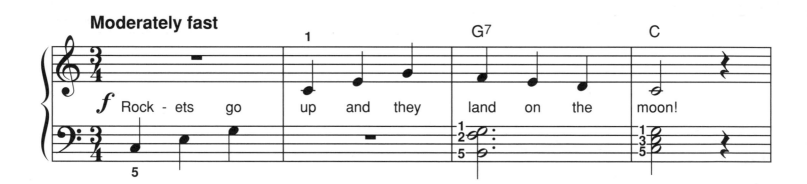

Rock - ets go up and they land on the moon!

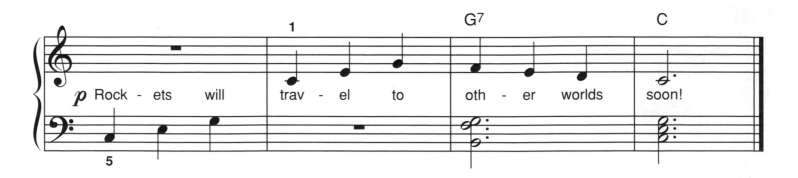

Rock - ets will trav - el to oth - er worlds soon!

IMPORTANT! Play *ROCKETS* again, playing the second line one octave (8 notes) higher. The rests at the end of the first line give you time to move your hands to the new position!

Play *ROCKETS* one more time, now with the first line one octave higher than written, and the second line two octaves higher.

This is excellent training in moving freely over the keyboard!

Slurs & Legato Playing

A **SLUR** is a curved line over or under notes on *different* lines or spaces.

SLURS mean play **LEGATO** (smoothly connected).

Slurs often divide the music into PHRASES.

A PHRASE is a musical thought or sentence.

WHAT CAN I SHARE?

90-102 = ♩

Moderately slow

mf

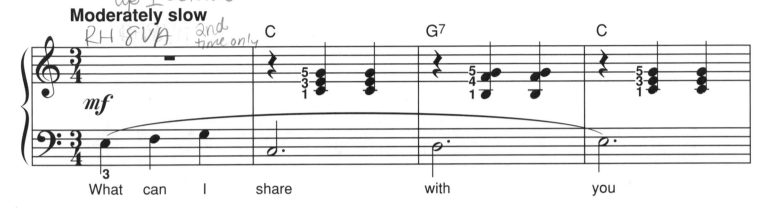

What can I share with you

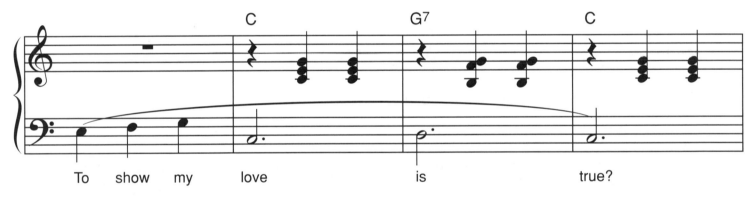

To show my love is true?

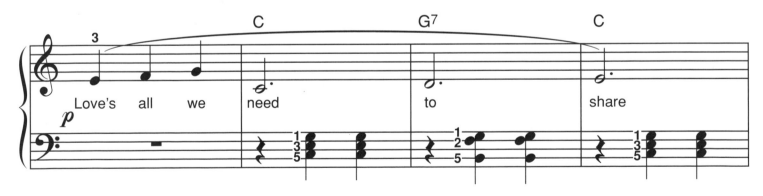

p

Love's all we need to share

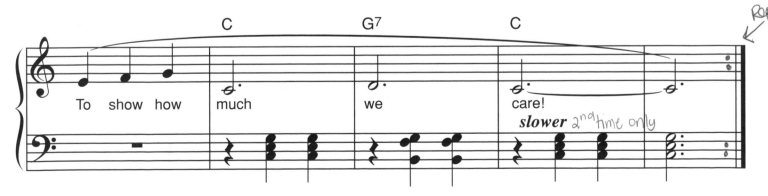

To show how much we care!

slower 2nd time only

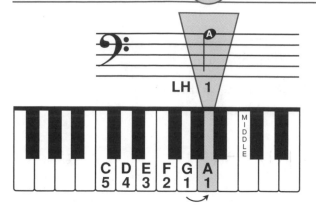

26

Introducing (A) for Left Hand

TO FIND A:

Place the LH in **C POSITION.**

Reach finger 1 one white key to the right!

Play slowly. Say the note names as you play.

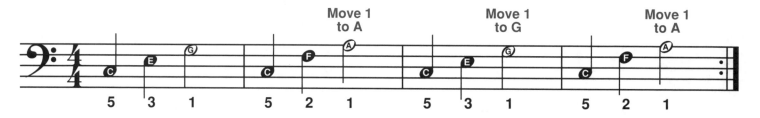

Introducing the F Major Chord

The C MAJOR chord is frequently followed by the F MAJOR chord, and vice-versa.

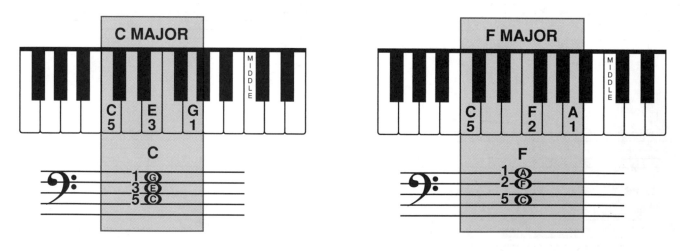

Practice changing from the C chord to the F chord and back again:

1. The 5th finger plays C in both chords.
2. The 2nd finger plays F in the F chord.
3. Only the 1st finger moves out of C POSITION (up to A) for the F chord.

Warm-Up using C, G⁷ & F Chords

Practice SLOWLY at first, then gradually increase speed.

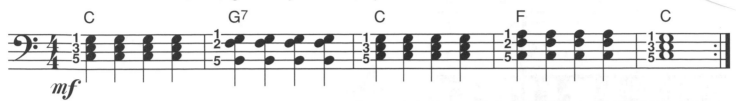

WHEN THE SAINTS GO MARCHING IN 🔊

(With RH MELODY & LH CHORDS)

> **INCOMPLETE MEASURE** Some pieces begin with an *incomplete measure.* The first measure of this piece has only 3 counts. The missing count is found in the last measure! When you repeat the whole song, you will have one whole measure of 4 counts when you play the last measure plus the first measure.

March time

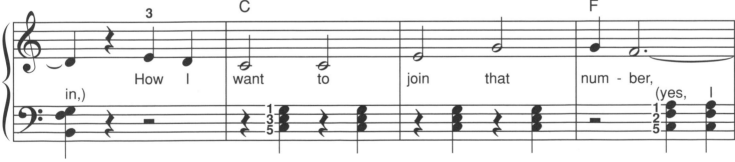

You are now ready to begin ADULT SACRED BOOK 1.

Introducing Ⓐ for Right Hand

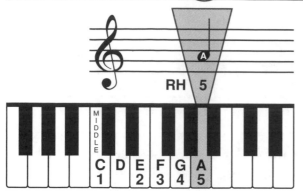

TO FIND A:

Place the RH in **C POSITION.**

Leave 1 on C.

Shift all other fingers one white key to the right!

Play slowly. Say the note names as you play.

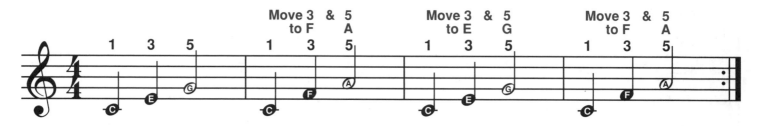

C & F Chords for Right Hand

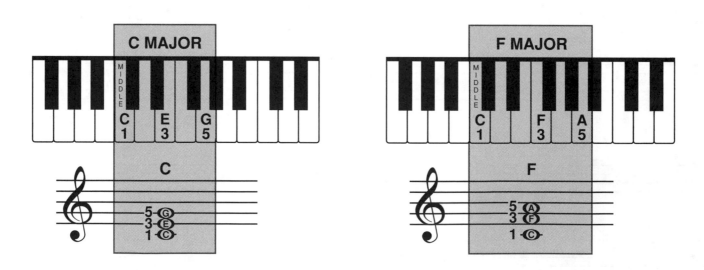

Practice changing from the C chord to the F chord and back again:
1. The 1st finger plays C in both chords.
2. The 3rd finger moves up to F and the 5th finger moves up to A for the F chord.

Warm-Up using C, G⁷ & F Chords

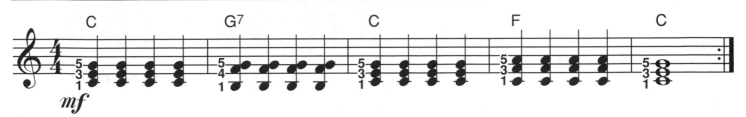

WHEN THE SAINTS GO MARCHING IN

(With LH MELODY & RH CHORDS)

After you have learned both versions of *WHEN THE SAINTS GO MARCHING IN,* you will find it very effective to play page 27 followed immediately by page 29. Instead of playing the piece one way and repeating, you will be playing the melody first in the RH, then in the LH!

You are now ready to begin ADULT CHRISTMAS BOOK 1.

G Position

Until now you have played
only in the C POSITION.

Now you will move to the G POSITION:

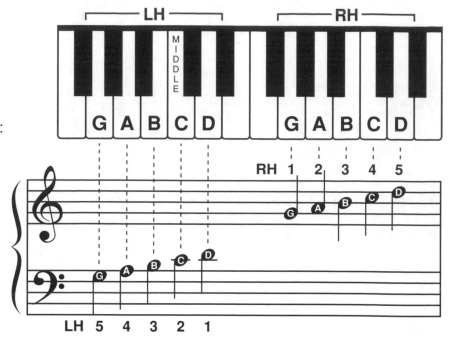

RH 1 on the G above middle C.

LH 5 on the G below middle C.

Play and say the note names. Be sure to do this SEVERAL TIMES!

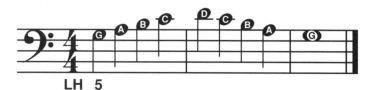 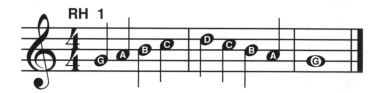

Intervals in G Position

1. **MELODIC INTERVALS**

   Say the name of each interval as you play.

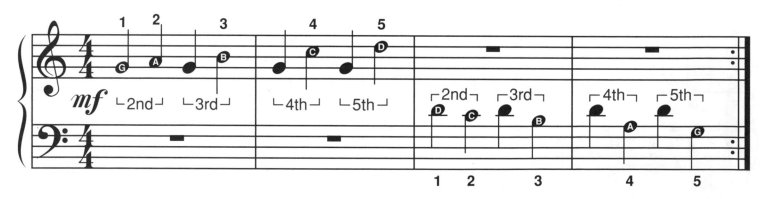

2. **HARMONIC INTERVALS**

   Say the name of each interval as you play.

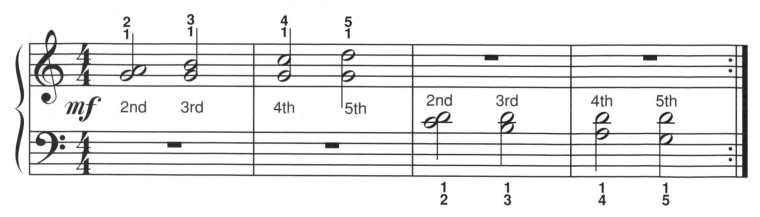

LOVE SOMEBODY! 24 🔊))

Before playing hands together, play LH alone, naming each harmonic interval!

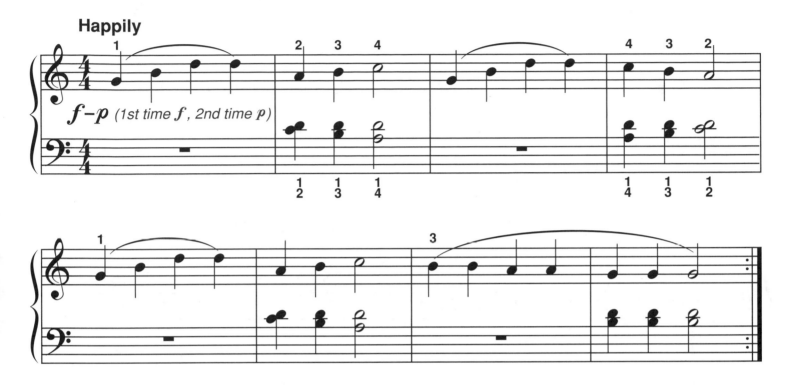

A FRIEND LIKE YOU 25 🔊))

Before playing hands together, play LH alone, naming each harmonic interval!

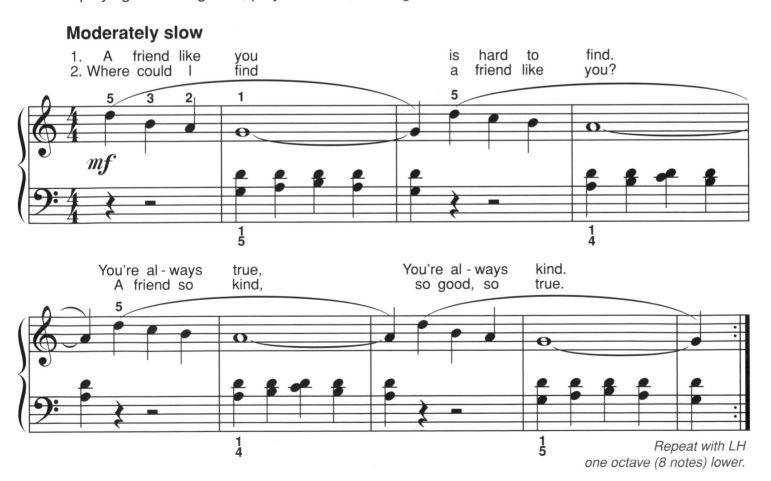

Repeat with LH one octave (8 notes) lower.

THE DONKEY 🔊

G POSITION

Before playing hands together, play LH alone, naming each harmonic interval.

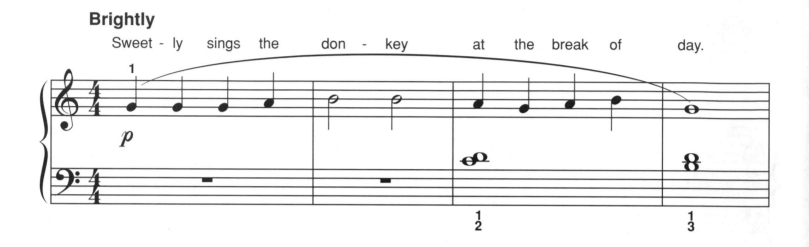

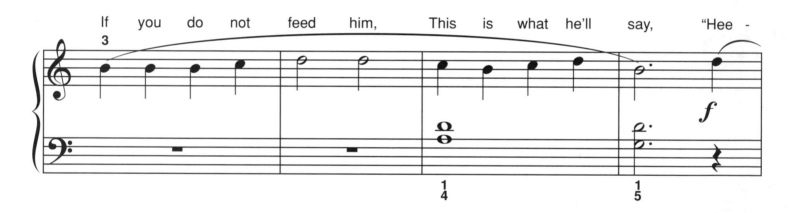

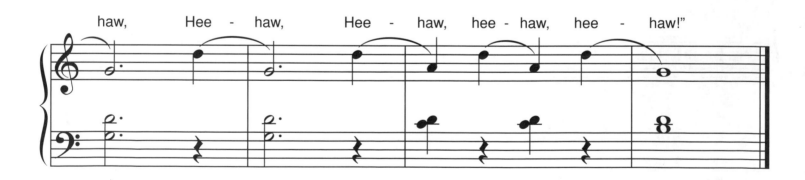

THE DONKEY may be played as a round for two to four pianos.

   The second piano begins after the first has played 4 measures.

   The third begins after the second has played 4 measures, etc.

Play 4 times.

The Sharp Sign

 The **SHARP SIGN** before a note means play the next key to the RIGHT, whether black or white!

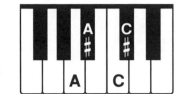

When a SHARP (♯) appears before a note, it applies to that note for the rest of the measure!

Circle the notes that are SHARP:

MONEY CAN'T BUY EV'RYTHING!

March time

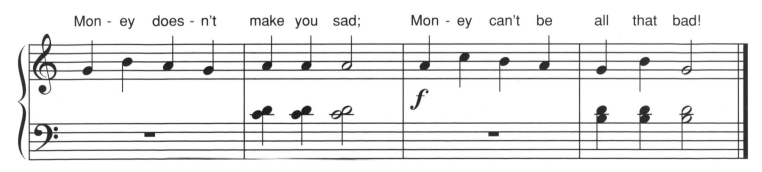

You are now ready to begin GREATEST HITS, Level 1, and CHRISTMAS HITS, Level 1.

The G Major & D⁷ Chords for Left Hand

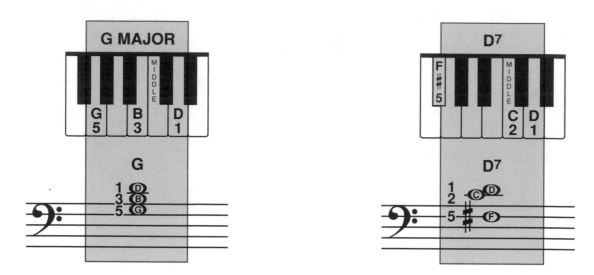

Practice changing from the G chord to the D⁷ chord and back again:

1. 1 plays D in both chords.
2. 2 plays C in the D⁷ chord.
3. Only 5 moves out of G POSITION (down to F♯) for D⁷.

Play the following several times.

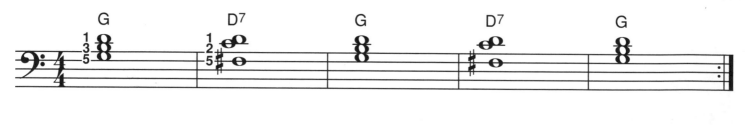

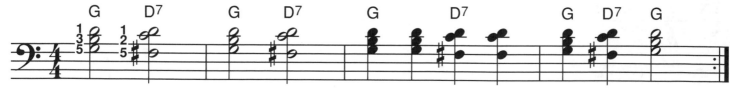

Preparation for *THE CUCKOO:*

THE CUCKOO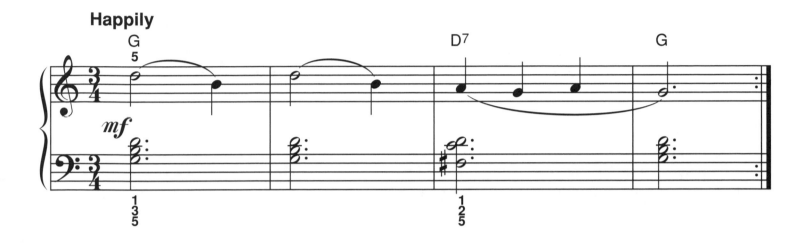

Happily

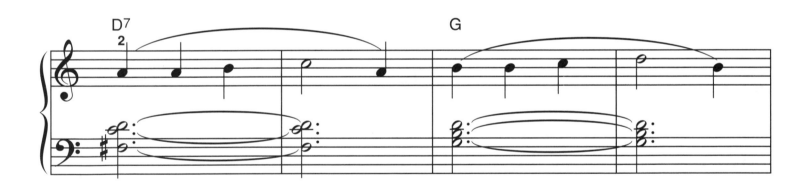

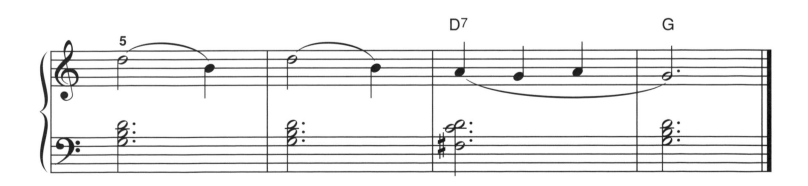

The G Major & D⁷ Chords for Right Hand

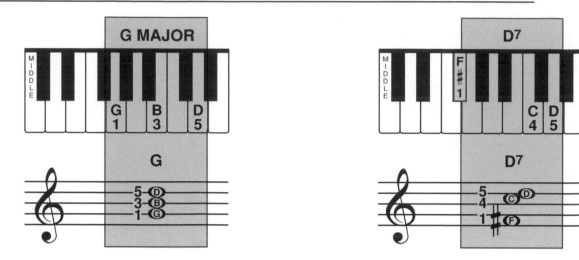

Practice changing from the G chord to the D⁷ chord and back again:

1. 5 plays D in both chords.
2. 4 plays C in the D⁷ chord.
3. Only 1 moves out of G POSITION (down to F♯) for D⁷.

Play several times:

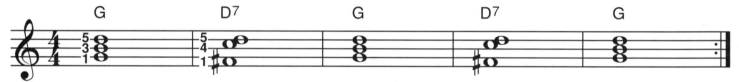

Block Chords & Broken Chords

When all three notes of a chord are played together, it is called a BLOCK chord.
When the three notes of a chord are played separately, it is called a BROKEN chord.
Play several times:

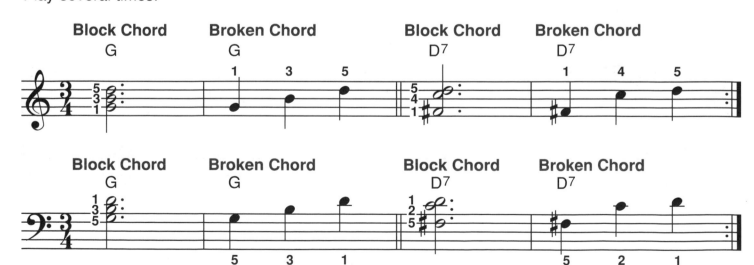

The Damper Pedal

- Use the RIGHT foot on the damper pedal.
- Always keep your heel on the floor.
- Use your ankle like a hinge.

The RIGHT pedal is called the **DAMPER** pedal.

When you hold the damper pedal down, any tone you sound will continue after you release the key.

This sign means: PEDAL DOWN   PEDAL UP

HOLD PEDAL

HARP SONG 🔊 29 Many pieces are made entirely of broken chords, as this one is!

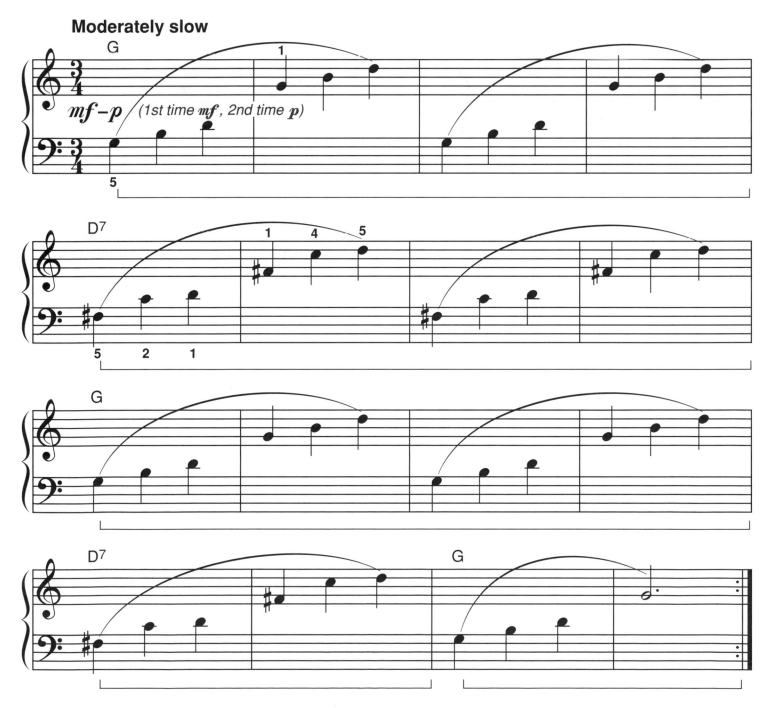

Also play *HARP SONG* in the following ways:

1. Play the third and fourth measures of each line one octave higher than written.
2. Play the first and second measures of each line one octave lower than written.

Introducing Ⓔ for Left Hand

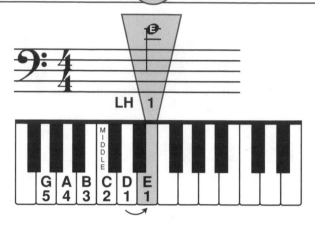

TO FIND E:

Place the LH in **G POSITION.**

Reach finger 1 one white key to the right!

Play slowly. Say the note names as you play.

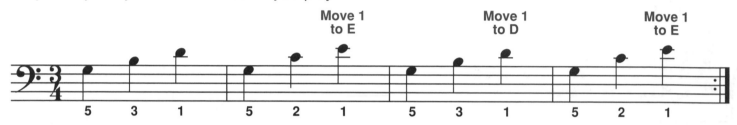

A New Position of the C Major Chord

You have already played the C MAJOR CHORD with C as the lowest note: **C E G.**

When you play these same three notes in any order, you still have a C MAJOR CHORD.
When you are playing in G POSITION, it is most convenient to play G as the lowest note: **G C E.**

The following diagrams show how easy it is to move from the G MAJOR CHORD to the
C MAJOR CHORD, when G is the lowest note of both chords.

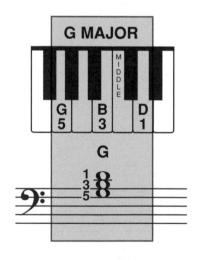

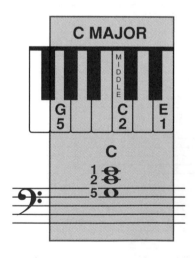

Practice changing from the G chord to the C chord and back again:

1. 5 plays G in both chords.
2. 2 plays C in the C chord.
3. Only 1 moves out of G POSITION (up to E) for the C chord.

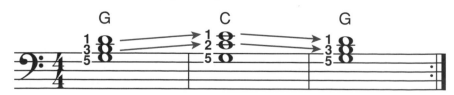

Warm-Up using G, D⁷ & C Chords

This warm-up introduces a new way of playing BROKEN CHORDS.

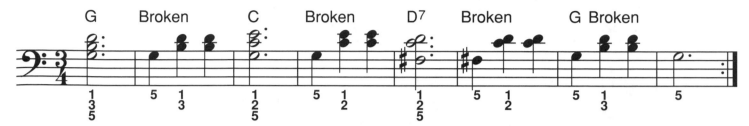

BEAUTIFUL BROWN EYES

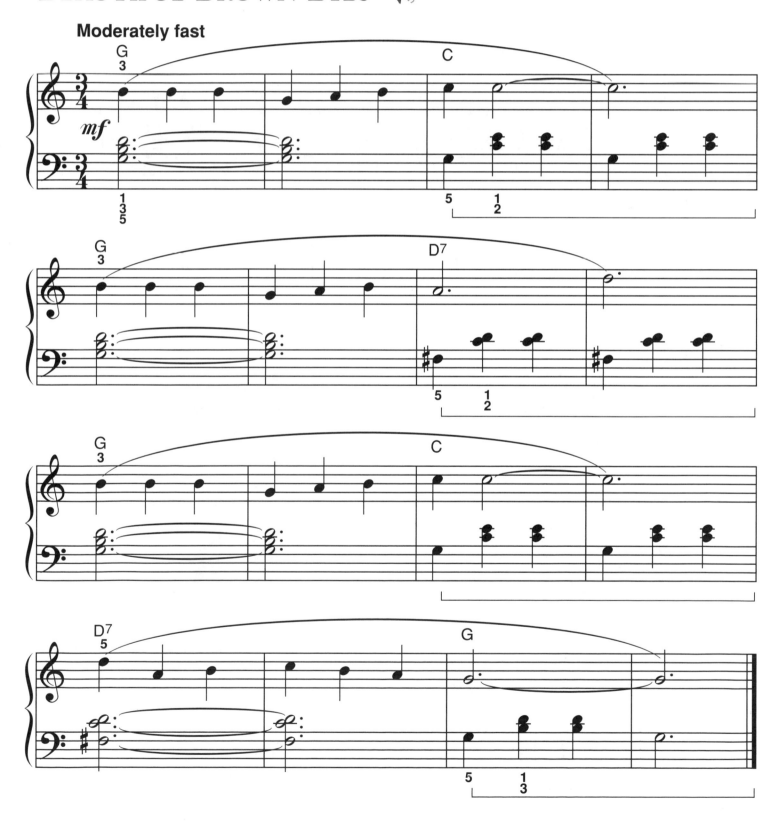

Introducing Ⓔ for Right Hand

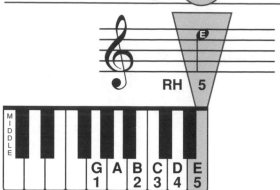

TO FIND E:

Place the RH in **G POSITION.**
Leave finger 1 on G.
Shift all other fingers one white key to the right.

Play slowly. Say the note names as you play.

New C Major Chord Position—Right Hand

Notice that *two* fingers must move to the right when changing from the G MAJOR CHORD to the C MAJOR CHORD.

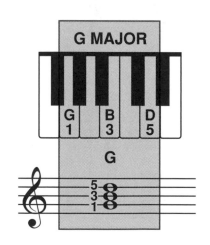

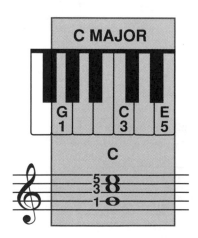

Practice changing from the G chord to the C chord and back again:

1. 1 plays G in both chords.
2. 3 moves up to C and 5 moves up to E for the C chord.

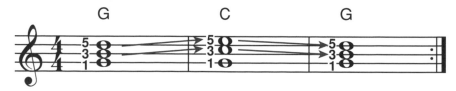

Warm-Up using G, D⁷ & C Chords

Play SLOWLY at first, then gradually increase speed.

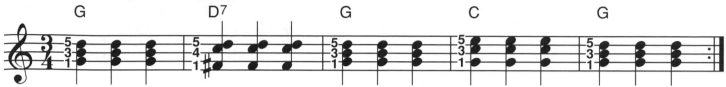

ALPINE MELODY 🔊

The LH melody of this piece consists entirely of BROKEN CHORDS,
which are the same as the BLOCK CHORDS played by the RH in each measure!

Moderately slow

*Play both hands 8va
(one octave higher)
the 2nd time!*

Middle C Position

The MIDDLE C POSITION uses notes you already know!

- RH is in C POSITION.
- LH moves one note down from G POSITION.
- Both thumbs are now on Middle C.

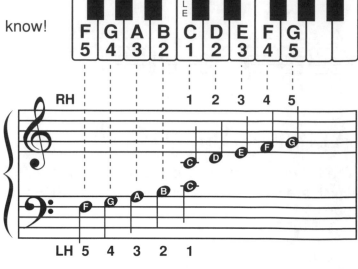

Play and say the note names. Do this several times!

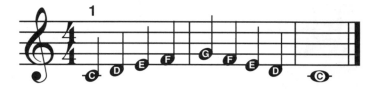

THUMBS ON C!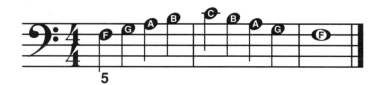

Moderately slow

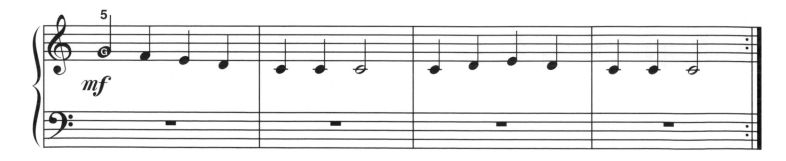

Waltz Time

NEW DYNAMIC SIGNS

Crescendo (gradually louder) *Diminuendo* (gradually softer)

CONTINUE TO READ BY PATTERNS! For LH, think:
"C, same, down a 2nd, down a 2nd, up a 2nd," etc.

Moderate waltz tempo (tempo = speed)

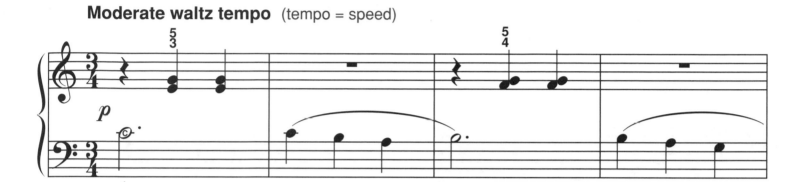

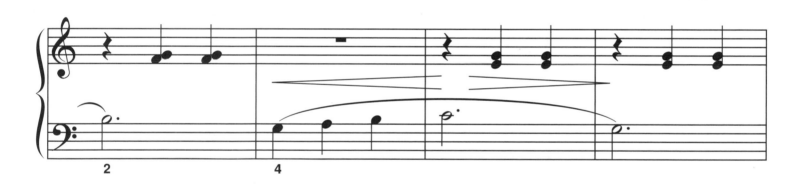

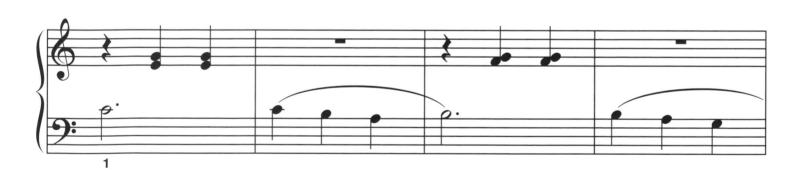

*Repeat with both hands 8va
(one octave higher).*

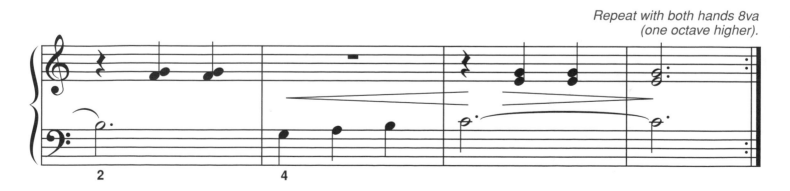

This sign is called a **FERMATA.**

Hold the note under the fermata *longer* than its value.

GOOD MORNING TO YOU!

MIDDLE C POSITION

Happily

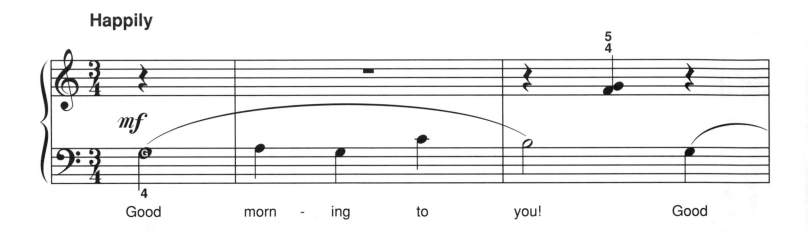

Good morn - ing to you! Good

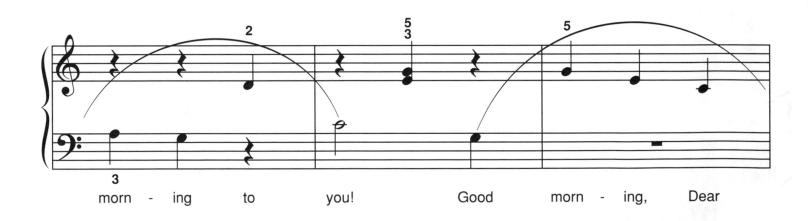

morn - ing to you! Good morn - ing, Dear

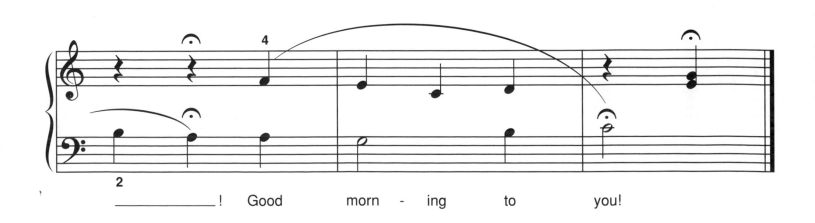

_____! Good morn - ing to you!

Eighth Notes

Two eighth notes are played in the time of **one quarter note.**

When a piece contains eighth notes, count:

"**1 - &**" or "**quar - ter**"   for each quarter note;

"**1 - &**" or "**two eighths**" for each pair of eighth notes.

Eighth notes
are usually played
in **pairs.**

COUNT: "**1   &**"

or: "**two eighths**"

Clap (or tap) these notes,
counting aloud:

HAPPY BIRTHDAY TO YOU! 🔊

HAPPY BIRTHDAY is exactly the same as *GOOD MORNING TO YOU,* except for the eighth notes!

Happily

You are now ready to begin ADULT POP SONG BOOK 1.

STANDING IN THE NEED OF PRAYER

For this popular spiritual, we return to C POSITION (LH 5 on C).

last measure-rest (handwritten)

double bar (handwritten)

Rhythmically, not too fast 90-102 (handwritten)

Copy, Paste to end (handwritten, left margin)

It's me! It's me, Oh Lord! Stand-ing in the need of prayer. It's

3 rests (handwritten)

(It's me!)

mf *f*

me! It's me, Oh Lord! Stand-ing in the need of prayer.

(It's me!)

Fine

combine w/ (handwritten)

Not my broth-er, not my sis-ter, but it's me, oh Lord! Stand-ing in the need of prayer. Not my

mf *f*

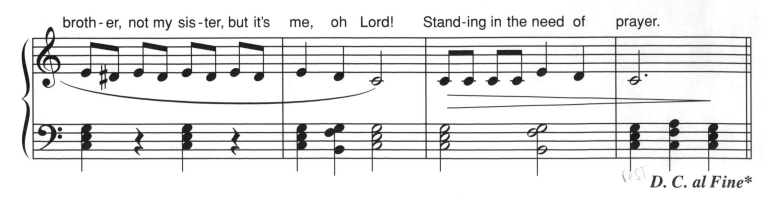

broth-er, not my sis-ter, but it's me, oh Lord! Stand-ing in the need of prayer.

rest (handwritten)

D. C. al Fine*

D. C. al Fine (Da Capo al Fine) means repeat from the beginning and play to the end (**Fine**).

THE GIFT TO BE SIMPLE 🔊

COMBINING MIDDLE C POSITION & C POSITION

You are now ready to play music that involves more than one position. This piece begins with the hands in MIDDLE C POSITION. After the first full measure is played, the LH moves to C POSITION to play chords. Change positions as indicated in the music.

This beautiful old Shaker melody was used by the famous American composer, Aaron Copland, in his well-known symphonic composition, *Appalachian Spring*.

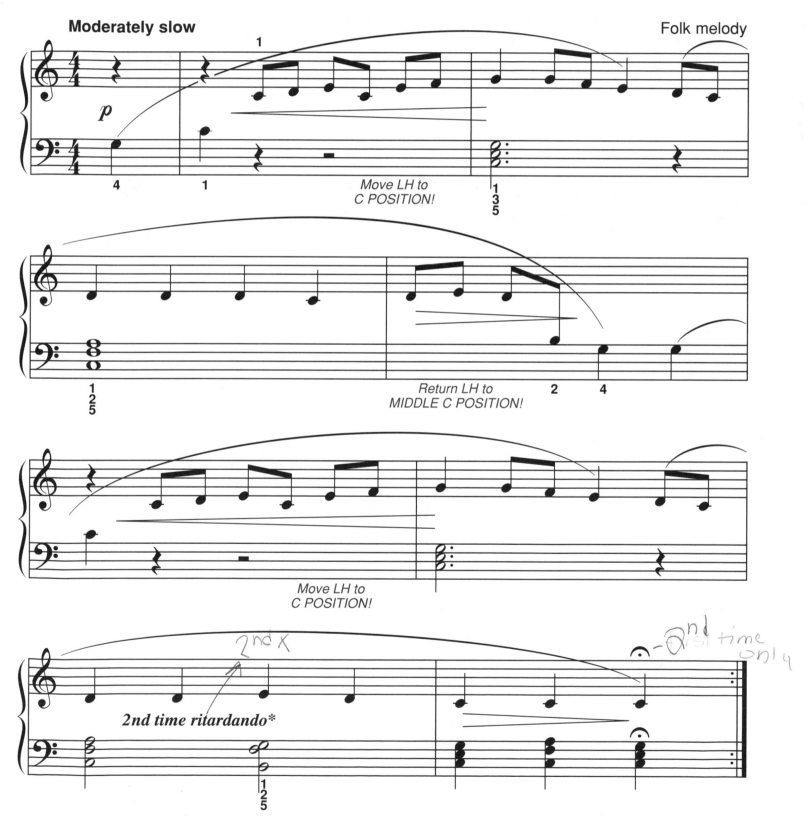

ritardando means *gradually slowing*.

Introducing Dotted Quarter Notes

A DOT INCREASES THE LENGTH OF A NOTE BY ONE HALF ITS VALUE.

A dotted half note is equal to a half note tied to a quarter note.

$$\text{2 COUNTS} + \text{1 COUNT} = \text{3 COUNTS}$$

A dotted quarter note is equal to a quarter note tied to an eighth note.

$$\text{1 COUNT} + \text{½ COUNT} = \text{1 ½ COUNTS}$$

Clap (or tap) the following rhythm. Clap **ONCE** for each note, counting aloud.

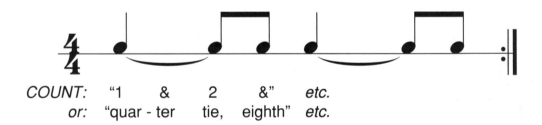

COUNT: "1 & 2 &" etc.
or: "quar - ter tie, eighth" etc.

The only difference between the following measure and the one directly above it is the way they are written. They are played the same.

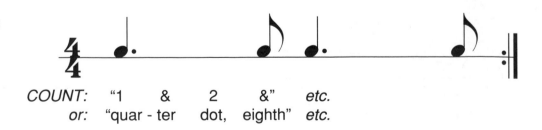

COUNT: "1 & 2 &" etc.
or: "quar - ter dot, eighth" etc.

In $\frac{4}{4}$ or $\frac{3}{4}$ time, the DOTTED QUARTER NOTE is almost *always* followed by an EIGHTH NOTE!

MEASURES FROM FAMILIAR SONGS USING DOTTED QUARTER NOTES

1. Count & clap (or tap) the notes. 2. Play & count. 3. Play & sing the words.

C POSITION

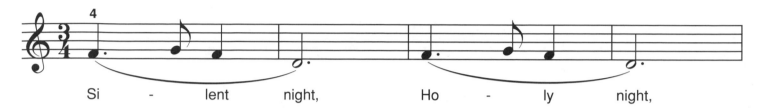

MIDDLE C POSITION (Both thumbs on Middle C)

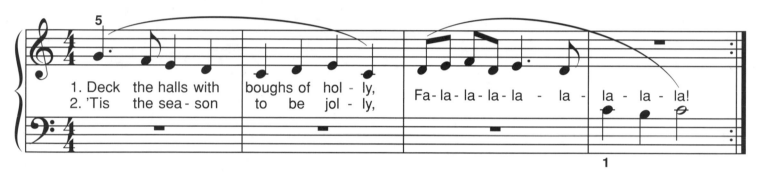

MIDDLE C POSITION

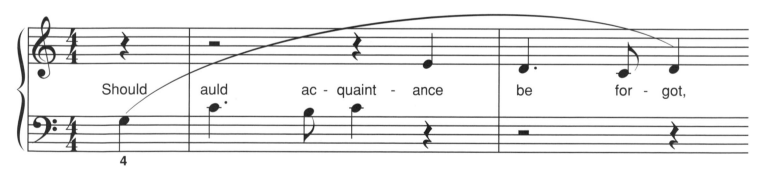

C POSITION

You are now ready to begin ADULT ALL-TIME FAVORITES, Book 1.

50

Alouette

C POSITION

Brightly

French folk song

Measuring 6ths

When you skip 4 white keys, the interval is a **6th**.

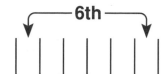

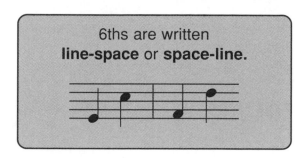

6ths are written
line-space or **space-line.**

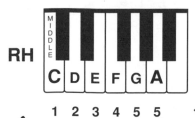

RH

This is C POSITION plus 1 note (A) played with 5.

RH 5 plays G or A!

Say the names of these intervals as you play!

MELODIC INTERVALS

2nd   3rd   4th   5th   6th

HARMONIC INTERVALS

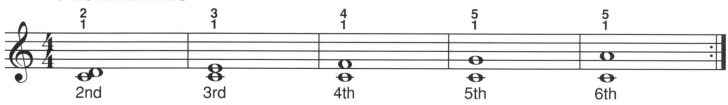

2nd   3rd   4th   5th   6th

LH

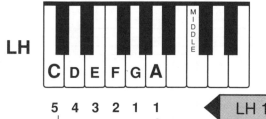

This is C POSITION plus 1 note (A) played with 1.

LH 1 plays G or A!

Say the names of these intervals as you play!

MELODIC INTERVALS

2nd   3rd   4th   5th   6th

HARMONIC INTERVALS

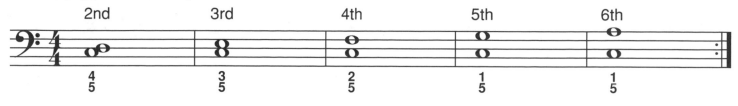

2nd   3rd   4th   5th   6th

In *LAVENDER'S BLUE,* 5ths and 6ths are played with 1 & 5.
Practice this warm-up before playing *LAVENDER'S BLUE.*

LAVENDER'S BLUE

C POSITION + 1

Moderately fast

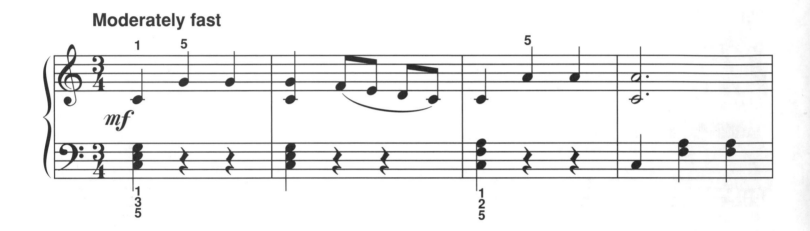

KUM-BA-YAH!*

WITH CHANGING TIME SIGNATURES

NEW TIME SIGNATURE

2/4 means **2** beats to each measure.

4 means a **QUARTER NOTE** ♩ gets one beat.

Moderately slow
2nd time both hands 8va

1. Kum - ba - yah, my Lord, Kum - ba - yah!
2. Some - one's pray - ing, Lord, Kum - ba - yah!

COUNT: 1 & 2 & 1 & 2 & 3 & 4 &

Kum - ba - yah, my Lord, Kum - ba - yah!
Some - one's pray - ing, Lord, Kum - ba - yah!

Kum - ba - yah, my Lord, Kum - ba - yah!
Some - one's pray - ing, Lord, Kum - ba - yah!

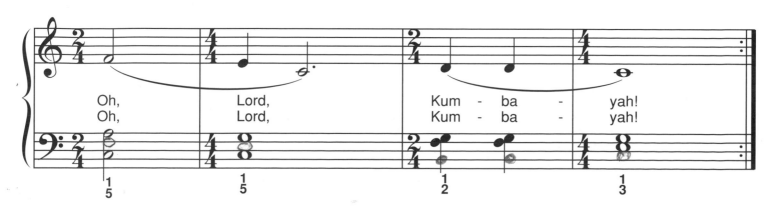

Oh, Lord, Kum - ba - yah!
Oh, Lord, Kum - ba - yah!

*Kum-ba-yah means "Come by here."

When you play in positions that include six or more notes, any finger may be required to play two notes.

LONDON BRIDGE

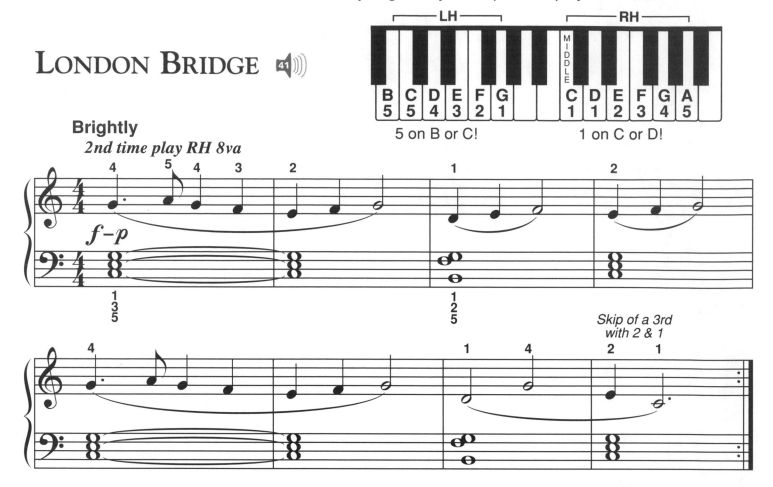

Brightly

2nd time play RH 8va

MICHAEL, ROW THE BOAT ASHORE

RH 1 plays C, RH 2 plays E.

Moderately slow

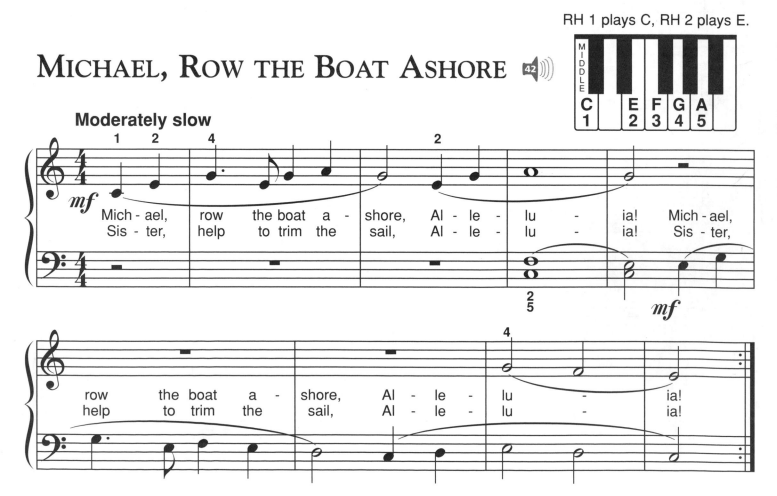

You are now ready to begin ADULT COUNTRY BOOK 1.

BLOW THE MAN DOWN!

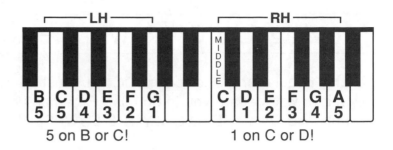

Moderately fast

Come all ye young fel - lows who fol - low the

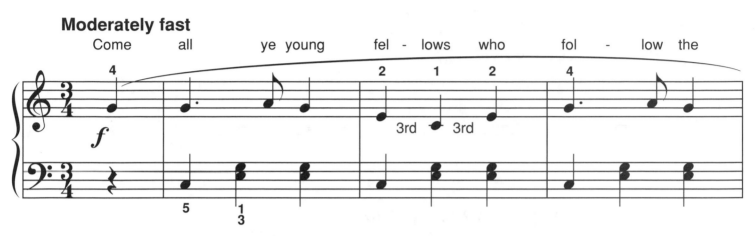

sea, Sing-ing "Way! Hey! Blow the man

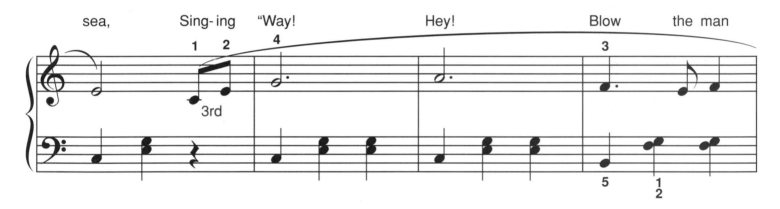

down!" And please pay at - ten - tion and lis - ten to

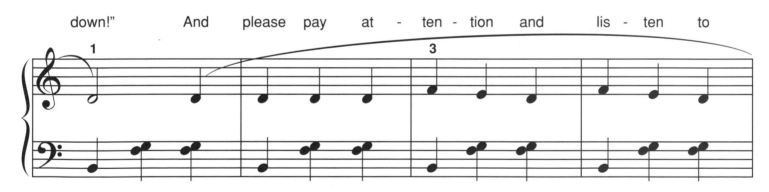

me; Give us some time to blow the man down!

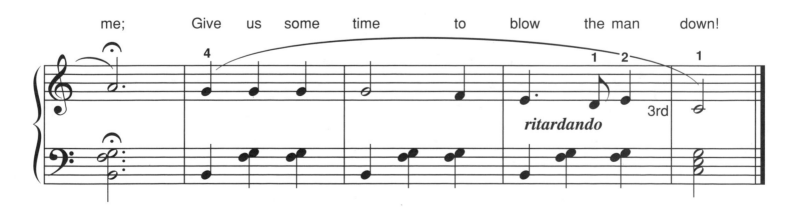

ritardando

Moving Up & Down the Keyboard in 6ths

To play popular and classical music, you must be able to move freely over the keyboard. These exercises will prepare you to do this. Each hand plays 6ths, moving up and down the keyboard to neighboring keys. READ ONLY THE LOWEST NOTE OF EACH INTERVAL, adding a 6th above!

RH 6ths, MOVING FROM  **UP TO** **AND BACK.**

Begin with RH 1 on MIDDLE C.

LH 6ths, MOVING FROM  **DOWN TO** **AND BACK.**

Begin with LH 1 on MIDDLE C.

LONE STAR WALTZ 🔊 44

This piece combines the positions used in *LONDON BRIDGE* with *Moving Up & Down the Keyboard in 6ths.*

Moderate waltz tempo
2nd time both hands 8va

2nd time ritardando

Fine

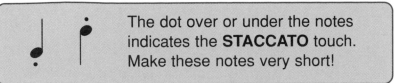

The dot over or under the notes indicates the **STACCATO** touch. Make these notes very short!

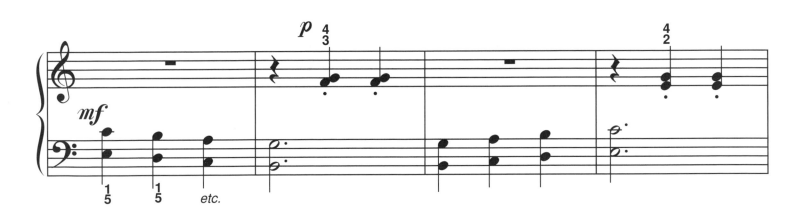

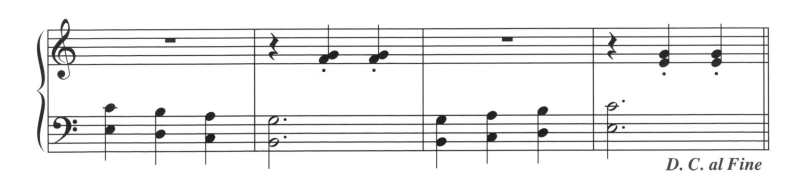

D. C. al Fine

Measuring 7ths & Octaves

When you skip 5 white keys,
the interval is a **7th**.

When you skip 6 white keys,
the interval is an **OCTAVE.**

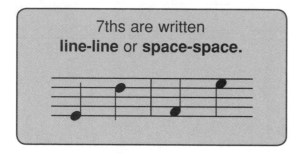

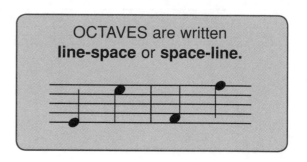

7ths are written
line-line or **space-space.**

OCTAVES are written
line-space or **space-line.**

Say the names of these intervals as you play!

RH MELODIC INTERVALS

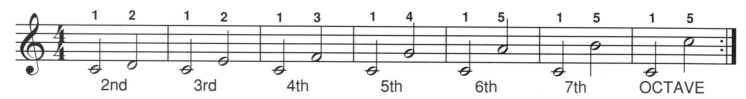

2nd　　3rd　　4th　　5th　　6th　　7th　　OCTAVE

RH HARMONIC INTERVALS

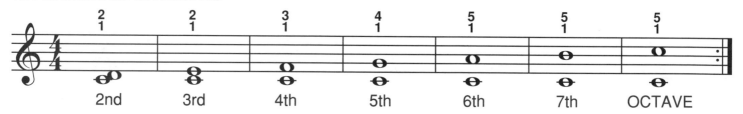

2nd　　3rd　　4th　　5th　　6th　　7th　　OCTAVE

LH MELODIC INTERVALS

LH HARMONIC INTERVALS

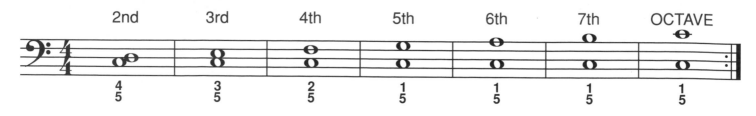

CAFÉ VIENNA 🔊

Play hands separately at first, then together.

Be especially careful of the RH fingering!

Notice that the first two notes, a melodic 3rd, are played with 2 & 1!

Moderate waltz tempo

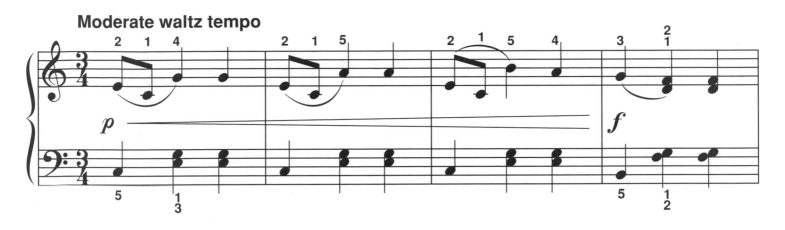

The Flat Sign

The **FLAT SIGN** before a note means play the next key to the LEFT, whether black or white!

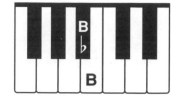

When a FLAT (♭) appears before a note, it applies to that note for the rest of the measure.

Circle the notes that are FLAT:

ROCK IT AWAY! 46

Moderately fast

If you're feel - in' blue, if you're feel - in' kind - a wear - y,

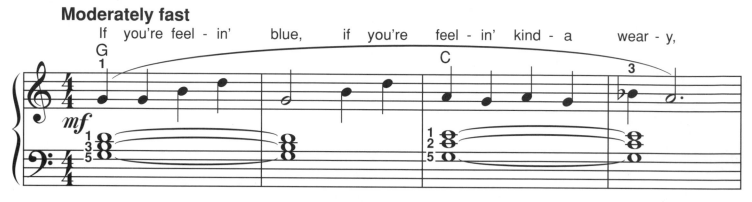

If you're feel - in' blue, bet - ter hear what I say!

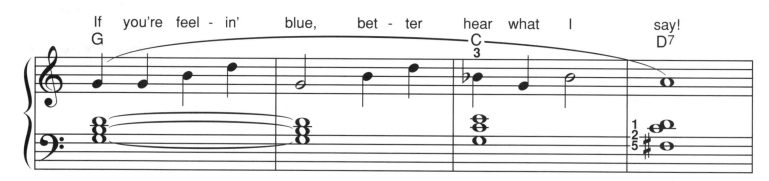

Play this rock - in' tune, it will sure - ly make you cheer - y;

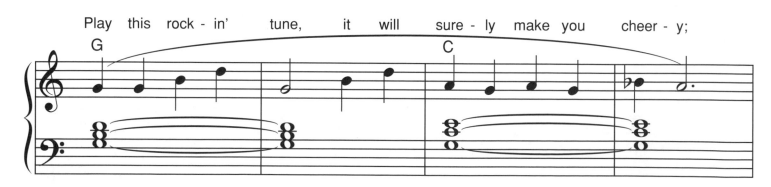

When you feel in trou - ble, just rock it a - way!

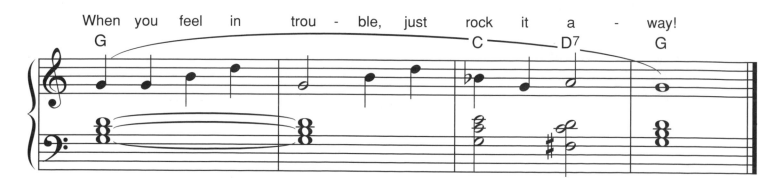

Measuring Half Steps & Whole Steps

Half Steps

A **HALF STEP** is the distance from any key to the very next key above or below (black or white).

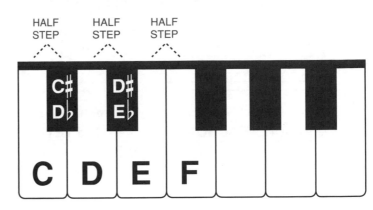

HALF STEPS · NO KEY BETWEEN

Whole Steps

A **WHOLE STEP** is equal to 2 half steps. Skip one key (black or white).

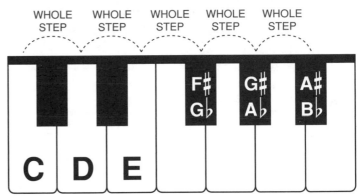

WHOLE STEPS · ONE KEY BETWEEN

Tetrachords

A **TETRACHORD** is a series of FOUR NOTES having a pattern of

WHOLE STEP, WHOLE STEP, HALF STEP.

The notes of a tetrachord must be in alphabetical order ➞

and must also have this pattern! ➞

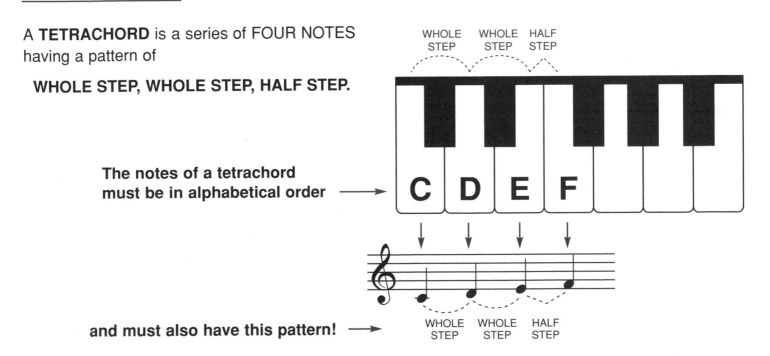

The Major Scale

The MAJOR SCALE is made of **TWO TETRACHORDS** *joined* by a **WHOLE STEP.**

The C MAJOR SCALE is constructed as follows:

There is no ♯ or ♭
in the **C MAJOR SCALE.**

Each scale begins and ends on a note of the same name as the scale, called the **KEY NOTE.**

Preparation for Scale Playing

IMPORTANT!   Since there are **8** notes in the C major scale and we only have **5** fingers,
an important trick must be mastered: **passing the thumb under the 3rd finger!**
This exercise will make this trick easy.

Play HANDS SEPARATELY. Begin VERY SLOWLY. Keep the wrist loose and quiet!

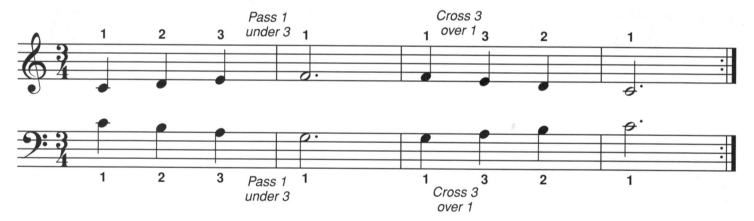

The C Major Scale

Begin SLOWLY. *Lean* the hand slightly in the direction you are moving.
The hand should move smoothly along, with no twisting motion of the wrist!

JOY TO THE WORLD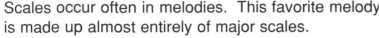

Scales occur often in melodies. This favorite melody is made up almost entirely of major scales.

NEW DYNAMIC SIGN

$\boldsymbol{ff}$ *(fortissimo)* = very loud

George Frideric Handel

Joyfully

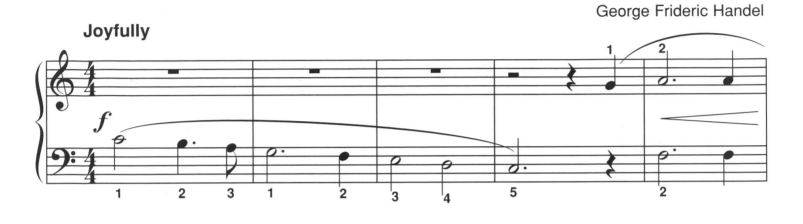

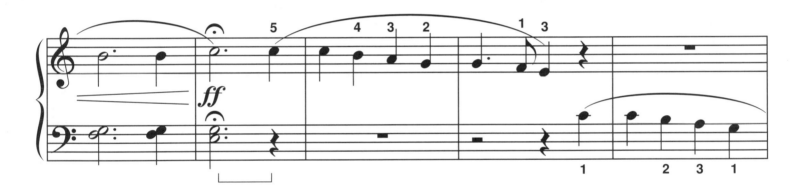

More About Chords

A TRIAD IS A 3-NOTE CHORD.

The three notes of a triad are:

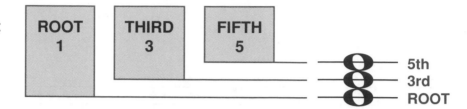

| ROOT 1 | THIRD 3 | FIFTH 5 |

— 5th
— 3rd
— ROOT

The ROOT is the note from which the triad gets its name. The root of a C triad is C.

Triads in **ROOT POSITION** (with root at the bottom) always look like this:

LINE — 5th
LINE — 3rd
LINE — ROOT

or this:

SPACE — 5th
SPACE — 3rd
SPACE — ROOT

> **Triads may be built on any note of any scale.**

TRIADS BUILT ON THE C MAJOR SCALE

Play with RH:

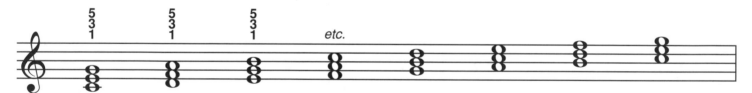

etc.

Play with LH:

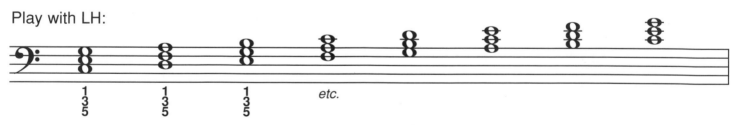

etc.

Listen carefully to the sound of these root position triads!

When you name the notes of any **TRIAD IN ROOT POSITION,** you will always skip **ONE** letter of the musical alphabet between each note. The triads you played above are:

C E G   D F A   E G B   F A C   G B D   A C E   B D F

This is the complete **"TRIAD VOCABULARY."** It should be memorized!

COCKLES AND MUSSELS

KEY OF C MAJOR
Key Signature: no ♯, no ♭

Music based on any particular scale is said to be in the **KEY** of that scale.

If there are sharps or flats in the scale, they are shown at the beginning of the music. This is called the **KEY SIGNATURE**.

The Primary Chords in C Major

The three most important chords in any key are those built on the 1st, 4th & 5th notes of the scale. These are called the **PRIMARY CHORDS** of the key.

The chords are identified by the Roman numerals **I**, **IV** & **V** (1, 4 & 5).

The **V** chord usually adds the note a 7th above the root to make a **V⁷** (say "5-7") chord.

In the key of C major, the **I CHORD** is the C MAJOR TRIAD.

The **IV CHORD** is the F MAJOR TRIAD.

The **V⁷ CHORD** is the G⁷ CHORD (G major triad with an added 7th).

The Primary Chords in C Major

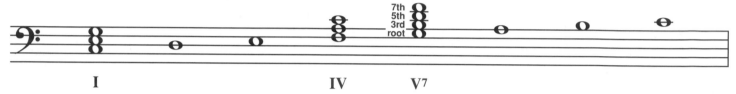

Chord Progressions

When we change from one chord to another, we call this a **CHORD PROGRESSION.**

When all chords are in root position, the hand must leap from one chord to the next. To make the chord progressions easier to play and sound better, the **IV** and **V⁷** chords may be played in other positions by moving one or more of the higher chord tones down an octave.

The **I** chord is played in ROOT POSITION:

The top note of the **IV** chord is moved down an octave:

In the **V⁷** chord, the 5th (D) is usually omitted. All notes except the root are moved down an octave:

The three PRIMARY CHORDS are then comfortably played as follows:

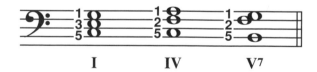

It is important that you now think of the C, F & G⁷ chords in the key of C MAJOR as the **I**, **IV** & **V⁷** chords!

Play the following line several times, saying the numerals of each chord as you play.

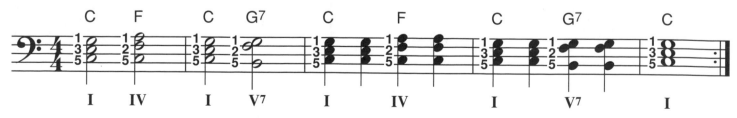

About the Blues

Music called **BLUES** has long been a part of the American musical heritage. We find it in the music of many popular song writers, in ballads, boogie, and rock.

BLUES music follows a basic formula, that is, a standard chord progression. If you learn the formula for *GOT THOSE BLUES!* you will be able to play the blues in any key you learn, simply by applying the formula to that key.

> **Formula for the Blues**
> There are 12 measures in one chorus of the blues:
>
>   4 measures of the **I** chord
>   2 measures of the **IV** chord
>   2 measures of the **I** chord
>   1 measure of the **V⁷** chord
>   1 measure of the **IV** chord
>   2 measures of the **I** chord

GOT THOSE BLUES! 49))

*The eighth notes may be played a bit unevenly:

long short long short, *etc.*

RH: An Extended Position

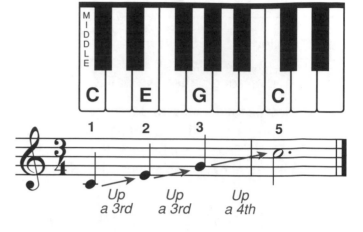

ON TOP OF OLD SMOKY begins and ends with the RH in an EXTENDED POSITION.

Play several times:

Up a 3rd   *Up a 3rd*   *Up a 4th*

LH Review: Block Chords & Broken Chords in C

BLOCK CHORDS

I   IV   V⁷

BROKEN CHORDS

I   IV   V⁷

ON TOP OF OLD SMOKY 🔊50

KEY OF C MAJOR
Key Signature: no ♯, no ♭

Moderately slow

EXTENDED POSITION

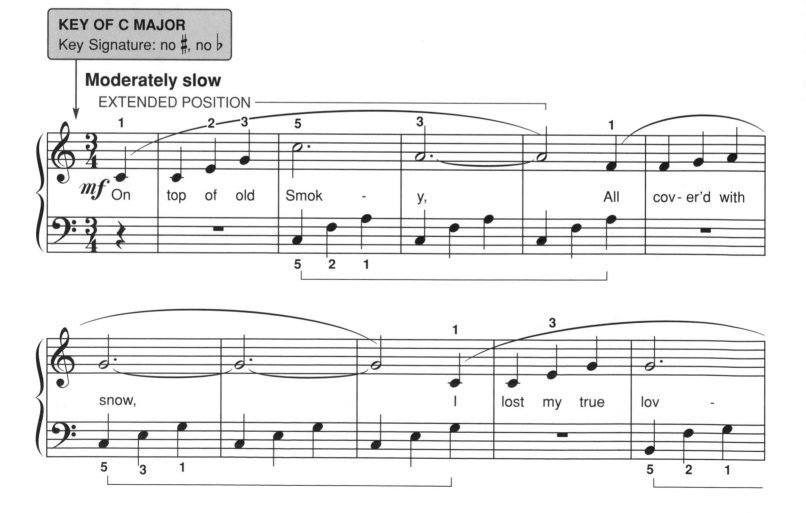

mf On top of old Smok - y,   All cov- er'd with

snow,   I lost my true lov -

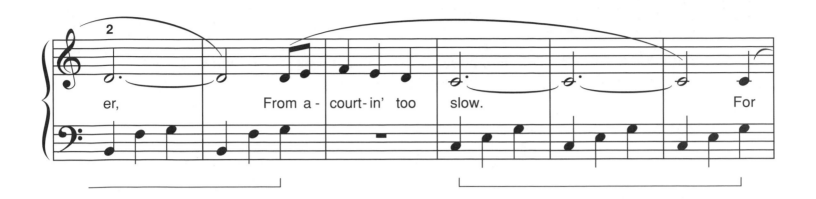

er, From a - court-in' too slow. For

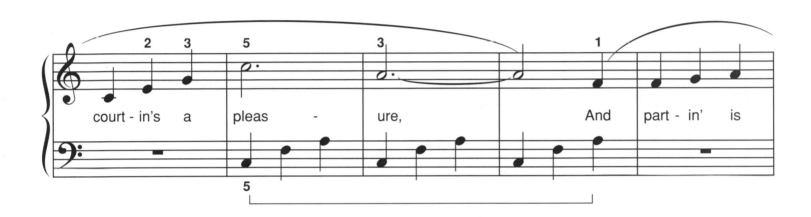

court - in's a pleas - ure, And part - in' is

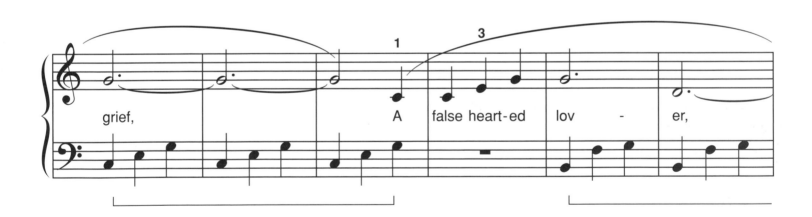

grief, A false heart-ed lov - er,

Is worse than a thief.

The G Major Scale

Remember that the MAJOR SCALE is made up of two tetrachords *joined* by a whole step.
The second TETRACHORD of the G MAJOR SCALE begins on D.

There is 1 sharp (F♯)
in the **G MAJOR SCALE.**

The Key of G Major

A piece based on the G major scale is in the **KEY OF G MAJOR.**
Since F is sharp in the G scale, every F will be sharp in the key of G major.

Instead of placing a sharp before every F in the entire piece,
the sharp is indicated at the beginning in the KEY SIGNATURE.

KEY OF G MAJOR
Key Signature: 1 sharp (F♯)
Play all "F's" sharp throughout.

Practice the G major scale with HANDS SEPARATE.
Begin SLOWLY. Keep the wrist loose and quiet.

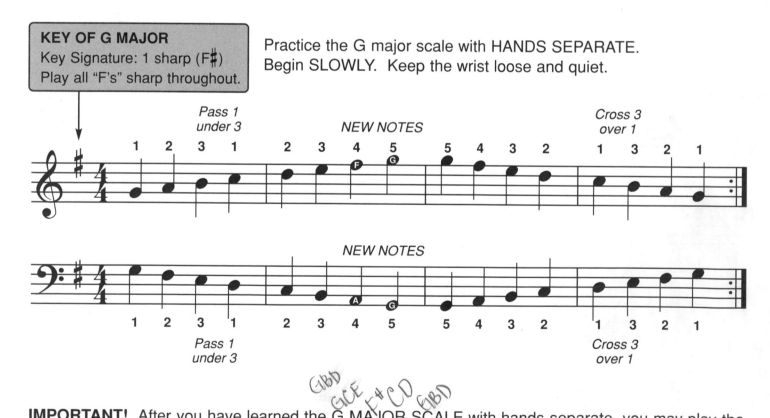

IMPORTANT! After you have learned the G MAJOR SCALE with hands separate, you may play the hands together. When the scale is played as written on the staffs above, the LH descends as the RH ascends, and vice versa. This is called CONTRARY MOTION—both hands play the *same numbered* fingers at the same time!

You may also play the C MAJOR SCALE at the bottom of page 62 with the hands together, in CONTRARY MOTION!

A New Trick!

CHANGING FINGERS ON THE SAME NOTE: Sometimes it is necessary to replay the same note with a different finger. Practice the following line to prepare for *THE CAN-CAN.*

THE CAN-CAN

KEY OF G MAJOR
Key Signature: 1 sharp (F♯)

Jacques Offenbach

*Descending G major scale

The Primary Chords in G Major

Reviewing the G MAJOR SCALE, LH ascending

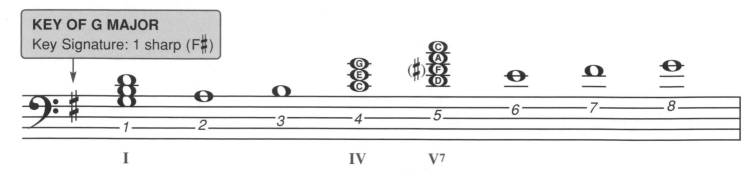

KEY OF G MAJOR
Key Signature: 1 sharp (F♯)

The following chord positions (which you have already learned) are used for smooth progressions:

Primary Chords in G

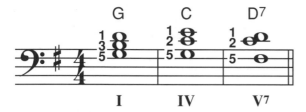

G Major Chord Progression with I, IV & V⁷ Chords

Play several times, saying the chord names and numerals aloud:

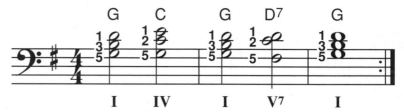

THE MARINES' HYMN 🔊

Moderate march tempo

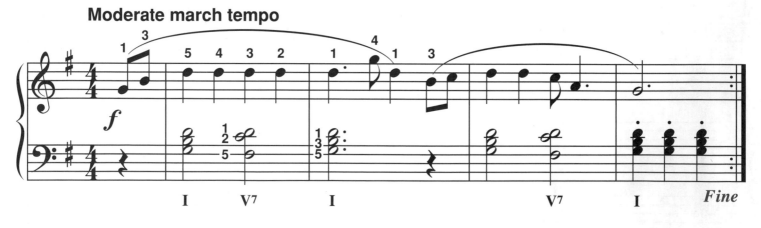

D. C. al Fine

Notes played between the main beats of the measure and held across the beat are called **SYNCOPATED NOTES.**

SYNCOPATED NOTE

COUNT: 1 & 2 & 3 & 4 &

WHY AM I BLUE?

The **NATURAL SIGN** cancels a sharp or flat!
A note after a natural sign is always a *white key!*

Moderately slow blues tempo

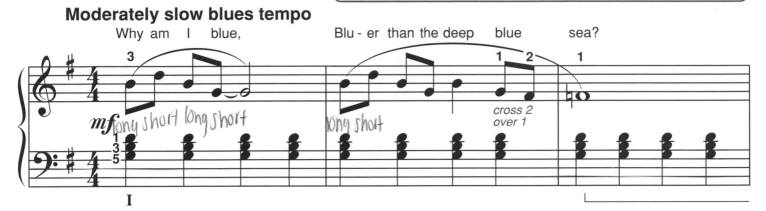

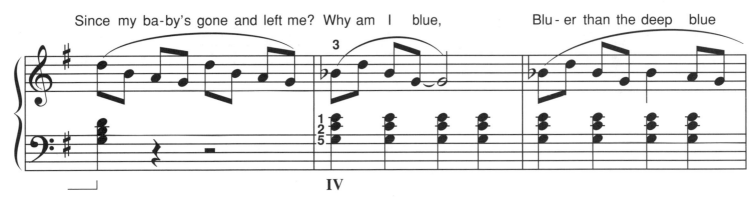

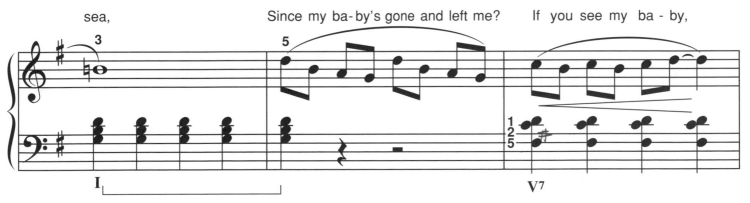

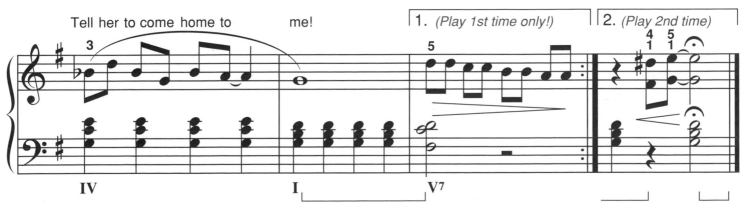

IMPORTANT! Compare the Roman numerals in this piece with those in *GOT THOSE BLUES*, on page 67.

You are now ready to begin the Adult JAZZ/ROCK Course.

The F Major Scale

There is 1 flat (B♭) in the **F MAJOR SCALE.**

The fingering for the F MAJOR SCALE with the LH is the same as for all the scales you have studied so far: 5 4 3 2 1 – 3 2 1 ascending; 1 2 3 – 1 2 3 4 5 descending.

Play slowly and carefully!

KEY OF F MAJOR
Key Signature: 1 flat (B♭)

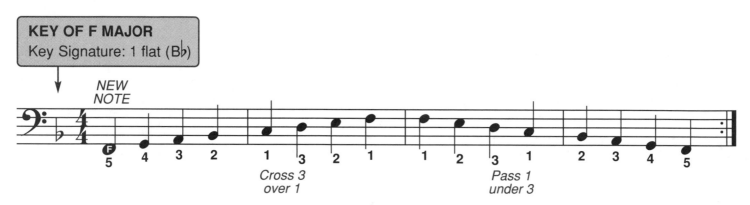

To play the F MAJOR SCALE with the RH, the 5th finger is not used! The fingers fall in the following groups: 1 2 3 4 – 1 2 3 4 ascending; 4 3 2 1 – 4 3 2 1 descending.

Play slowly and carefully!

As soon as you play the thumb, move it under, carrying it at the base of the 3rd and 4th fingers until it is needed. Keep the wrist even, and move the hand smoothly along. Never twist the wrist when the thumb goes under.

Practice the F major scale several times daily. Begin slowly and gradually increase speed.
Play only with HANDS SEPARATE:

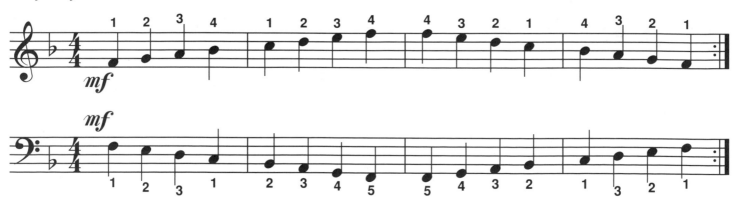

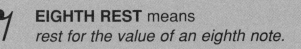

EIGHTH REST means
rest for the value of an eighth note.

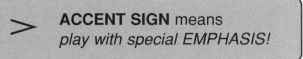

ACCENT SIGN means
play with special EMPHASIS!

LITTLE BROWN JUG

American folk song

The Primary Chords in F Major

Reviewing the F MAJOR SCALE, LH ascending

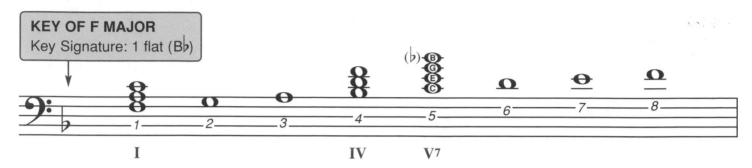

The following chord positions are often used for smooth progressions:

Primary Chords in F

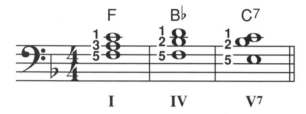

F Major Chord Progression with I, IV & V7 Chords

Play several times, saying the chord names and numerals aloud:

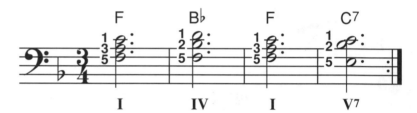

CHIAPANECAS (Mexican Hand-Clapping Song) 🔊

Moderately fast

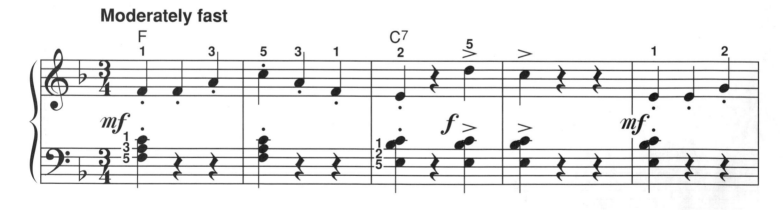

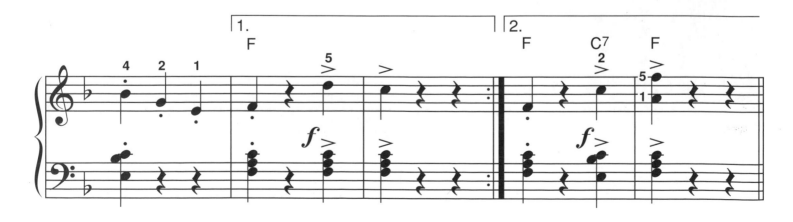

The double dots inside the double bars indicate that everything between the double bars must be REPEATED.

A New Style of Bass

Play this several times before beginning *O SOLE MIO:*

Moderately slow

COUNT: 1 & 2 & 3 & 4 &   1 & 2 & 3 & 4 &   1 & 2 & 3 & 4 &   1 & 2 & 3 & 4 &

O Sole Mio!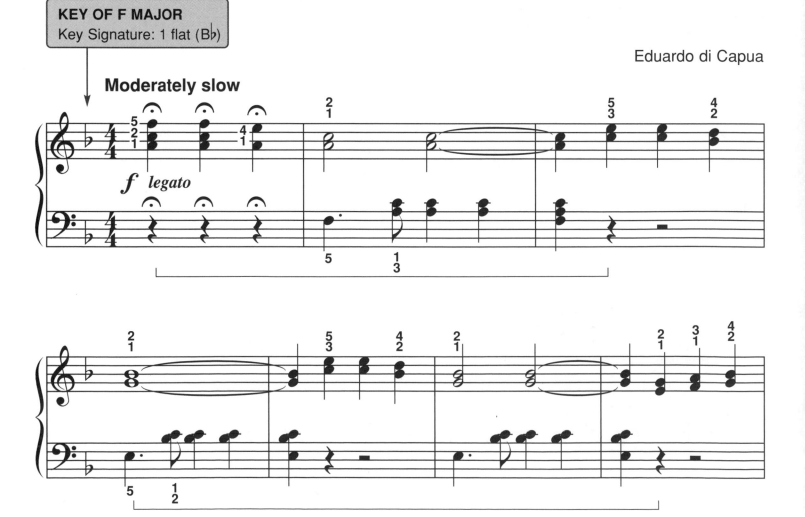

From Enrico Caruso to a recording entitled "In Concert," by José Carreras, Placido Domingo and Luciano Pavarotti, this great old favorite has provided tenors with surefire encore material. "There's No Tomorrow," popular in the 50s and 60s, was sung to this melody.

KEY OF F MAJOR
Key Signature: 1 flat (B♭)

Eduardo di Capua

Moderately slow

*Note the D♭ in the B♭ chord. This changes the **IV** chord to a MINOR chord, as will be explained later.

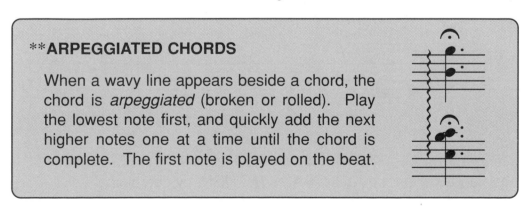

**ARPEGGIATED CHORDS

When a wavy line appears beside a chord, the chord is *arpeggiated* (broken or rolled). Play the lowest note first, and quickly add the next higher notes one at a time until the chord is complete. The first note is played on the beat.

The Key of A Minor (Relative of C Major)

Every MAJOR key has a **RELATIVE MINOR** key that has the same KEY SIGNATURE.

The RELATIVE MINOR begins on the **6th** tone of the MAJOR scale.
The RELATIVE MINOR of C MAJOR is, therefore, A MINOR.

C MAJOR SCALE

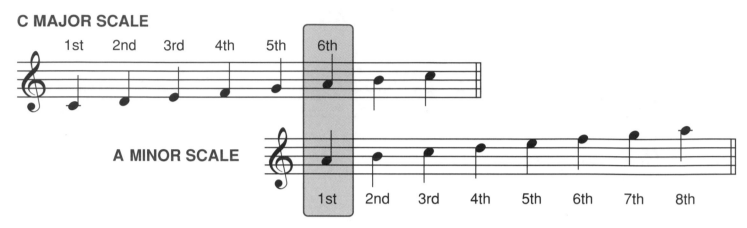

Because the keys of C MAJOR and A MINOR have the same KEY SIGNATURE (no sharps, no flats), they are RELATIVES.

The minor scale shown above is called the **NATURAL MINOR SCALE.**
It uses only notes that are found in the relative major scale.

The A Harmonic Minor Scale

The most frequently used MINOR SCALE is the **HARMONIC MINOR.** In this scale, the 7th tone is raised ascending and descending.

The raised 7th in the key of A MINOR is G♯. It is not included in the key signature, but is written in as an "accidental" sharp each time it occurs.

Practice the A HARMONIC MINOR SCALE with hands separate. Begin slowly.

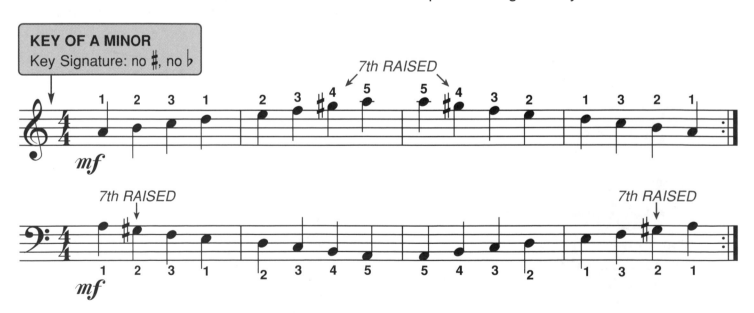

IMPORTANT! After you have learned the A HARMONIC MINOR SCALE with hands separate, you may play the hands together in CONTRARY MOTION, by combining the two staffs above.

MORE SYNCOPATED NOTES:

JERICHO

KEY OF A MINOR
Key Signature: no ♯, no ♭*

See how many syncopated notes you can find in *JERICHO.*

*To determine whether a piece is in a major key or its relative minor, look at the end of the piece. It will end on the key note or chord. This piece has no sharps or flats in the key signature and it ends on A (an A MINOR chord); therefore, the piece is in the key of A MINOR.

Introducing "Overlapping Pedal"

The following sign is used to indicate OVERLAPPING PEDAL.

At this point, pedal again.

PLAY

PED UP / PED DOWN

As the hand goes *down,*
the foot comes *up.*
Pedal again immediately.

Practice the following exercises before playing *GREENSLEEVES.*

GREENSLEEVES 🔊 58

KEY OF A MINOR
Key Signature: no ♯, no ♭

NEW DYNAMIC SIGN

mp *(mezzo piano)* = medium soft

Moderately slow

mp

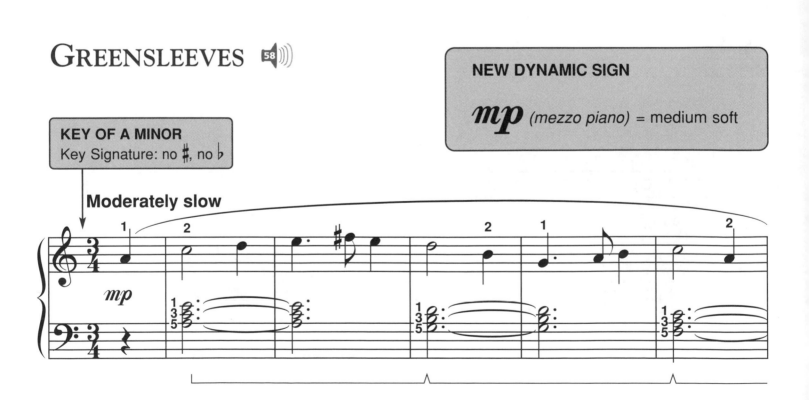

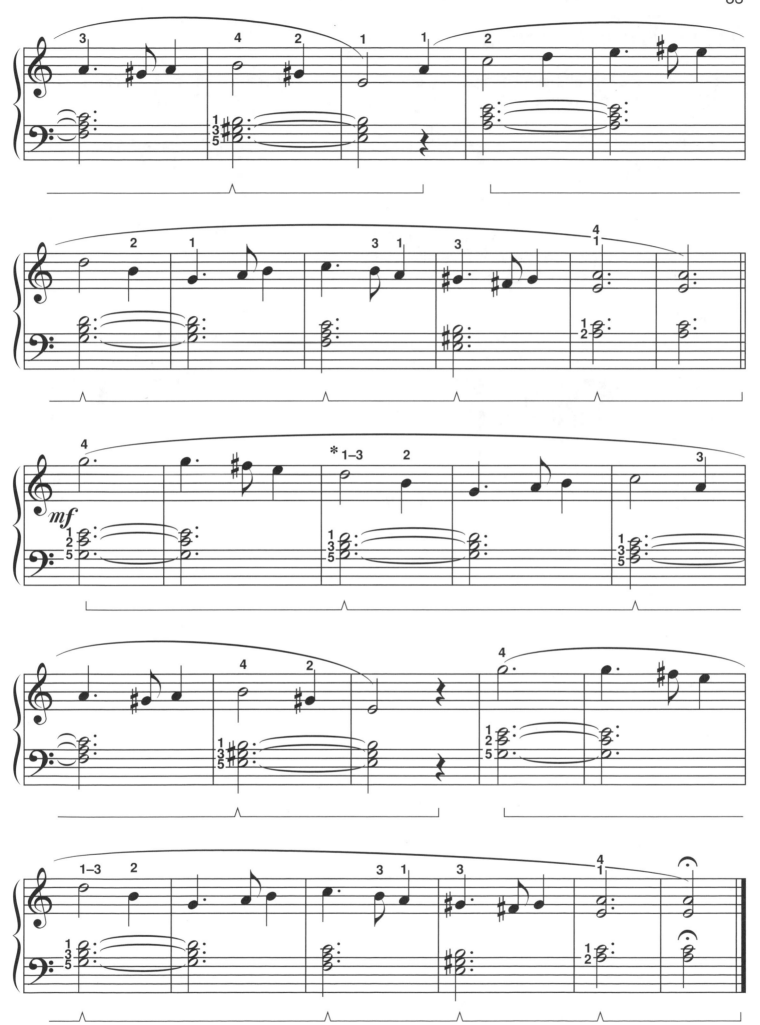

*FINGER SUBSTITUTION: While holding the note down with 1, change to 3 on the 2nd beat.

More About Triads

1. Some of the 3rds you have been playing are MAJOR 3rds, and some are MINOR (smaller) 3rds.

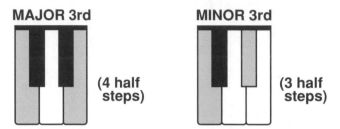

MAJOR 3rd (4 half steps)   **MINOR 3rd** (3 half steps)

Any MAJOR 3rd may be changed to a MINOR 3rd by lowering the upper note one half step!

2. All of the 5ths you have played so far are PERFECT 5ths.

PERFECT 5th (7 half steps)

3. MAJOR TRIADS consist of a ROOT, MAJOR 3rd & PERFECT 5th.

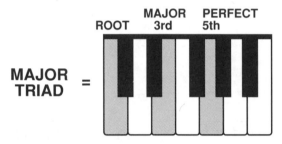

MAJOR TRIAD = ROOT, MAJOR 3rd, PERFECT 5th

4. MINOR TRIADS consist of a ROOT, MINOR 3rd & PERFECT 5th.

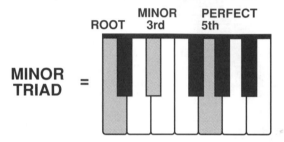

MINOR TRIAD = ROOT, MINOR 3rd, PERFECT 5th

Any MAJOR triad may be changed to a MINOR triad by lowering the 3rd one half step!

5. Play the following triads with RH 1 3 5. Say "C major triad, C minor triad," etc., as you play each pair. Then repeat ONE OCTAVE LOWER, using LH 5 3 1.

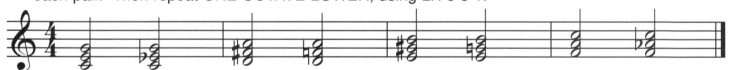

The Primary Chords in A Minor

Reviewing the A HARMONIC MINOR SCALE, LH ascending

Small (lower case) Roman numerals are used to indicate minor triads (i & iv).

Small (lower case) m = minor

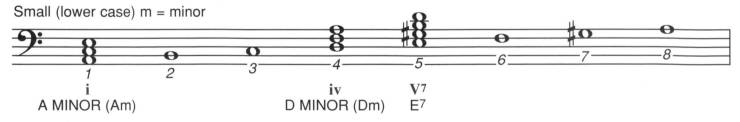

i — A MINOR (Am)   iv — D MINOR (Dm)   V7 — E7

The following positions are often used for smooth progressions:

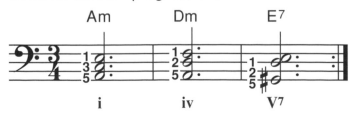

Am   Dm   E7
i   iv   V7

The same, one octave higher.

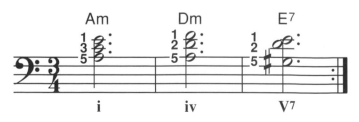

Am   Dm   E7
i   iv   V7

Go Down, Moses 59

KEY OF A MINOR
Key Signature: no ♯, no ♭

Moderately slow

When Is - rael was in E - gypt's land, Let my peo - ple go! Op -

pressed so hard they could not stand, Let my peo - ple go!

Go down, Mos - es, 'Way down in E - gypt's land,

Tell old Pha - raoh, Let my peo - ple go.

The Key of D Minor (Relative of F Major)

D MINOR is the relative of **F MAJOR.**

Both keys have the same key signature (1 flat, B♭).

REMEMBER: The RELATIVE MINOR begins on the **6th** tone of the major scale.
The relative minor of F MAJOR is, therefore, D MINOR.

F MAJOR SCALE

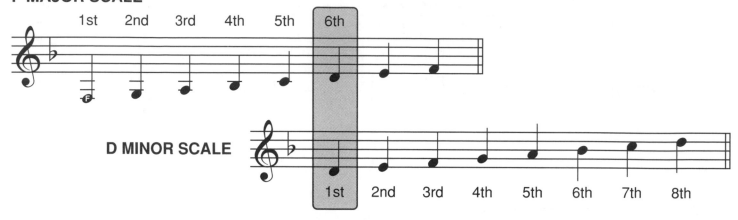

The minor scale shown above is the NATURAL MINOR scale. Remember, the natural minor uses only notes that are found in the relative major scale.

The D Harmonic Minor Scale

In the HARMONIC MINOR scale, the 7th tone is raised ascending and descending.

The raised 7th in the key of D MINOR is C♯. It is not included in the key signature, but is written as an "accidental" sharp each time it occurs.

Practice the D HARMONIC MINOR scale with hands separate. Begin slowly.

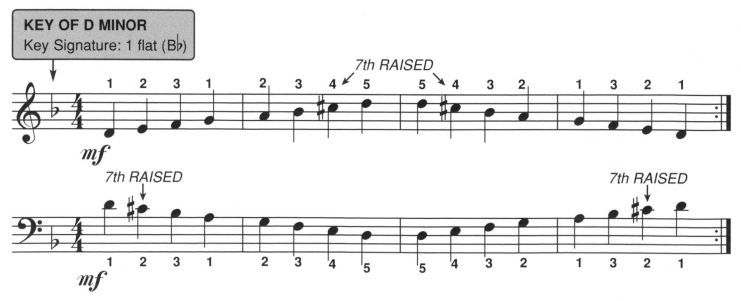

IMPORTANT! After you have learned the D HARMONIC MINOR SCALE with hands separate, you may play the hands together in CONTRARY MOTION, by combining the two staffs above.

Scarborough Fair

60

NEW DYNAMIC SIGN

pp *(pianissimo)* = very soft

KEY OF D MINOR
Key Signature: 1 flat (B♭)

2nd time 8va

Are you goin' to Scar - bor - ough fair? Pars - ley, sage, Rose - mar - y and thyme. Re - mem - ber me to one who lives there. She was once a true love of mine.

The Primary Chords in D Minor

Reviewing the D HARMONIC MINOR SCALE, LH ascending

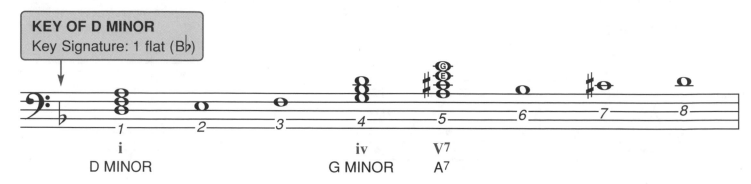

KEY OF D MINOR
Key Signature: 1 flat (B♭)

i
D MINOR

iv
G MINOR

V7
A7

The following positions are often used for smooth progressions:

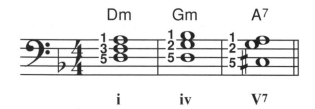

Dm   Gm   A7

i   iv   V7

Play several times, saying the chord names and numerals aloud:

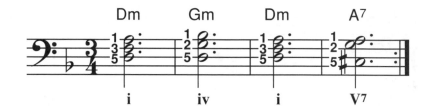

Dm   Gm   Dm   A7

i   iv   i   V7

D MINOR PROGRESSION with broken i, iv & V7 chords

Play several times.

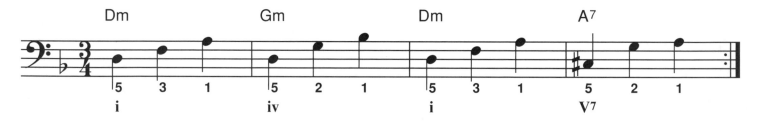

Dm   Gm   Dm   A7

i   iv   i   V7

RAISINS AND ALMONDS 🔊61

Folk song

Moderately

mf When I was a ti-ny sleep-y - head, Ma - ma

mp

90

HE'S GOT THE WHOLE WORLD IN HIS HANDS

This piece reviews the **I**, **IV** & **V^7** chords of the keys of G MAJOR, C MAJOR and F MAJOR.
It also reviews syncopated notes, in preparation for *THE ENTERTAINER,* on pages 92–93.

KEY OF G MAJOR
Key Signature: 1 sharp (F♯)

Moderately & rhythmically

Spiritual

KEY OF C MAJOR
Key Signature: no ♯, no ♭

KEY OF F MAJOR
Key Signature: 1 flat (B♭)

ritardando

(A - men!)

LH Warm-Up

Practice many times, very slowly. These four measures contain everything new that you will find in the LH of *THE ENTERTAINER!*

THE ENTERTAINER 🔊 *Only Play Once*

Scott Joplin

Not fast!*

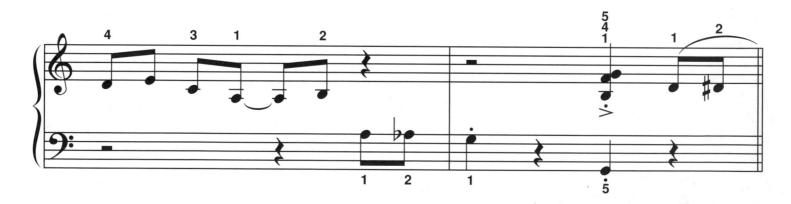

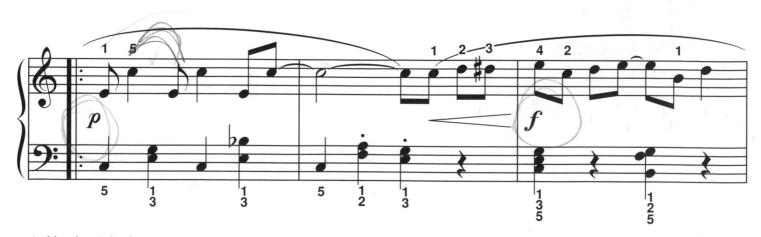

* "Not fast" is the composer's own indication!

Eighth Note Triplets

When three notes are grouped together with a figure "*3*" above or below the notes, the group is called a **TRIPLET.**

The three notes of an eighth-note triplet group = one quarter note.

When a piece contains triplets, count **"trip-a-let"**

or **"one & then"**

or any way suggested by your teacher.

AMAZING GRACE

John Newton, J. Carrell & D. Clayton
Arr. by P. M. & L.

Moderately slow

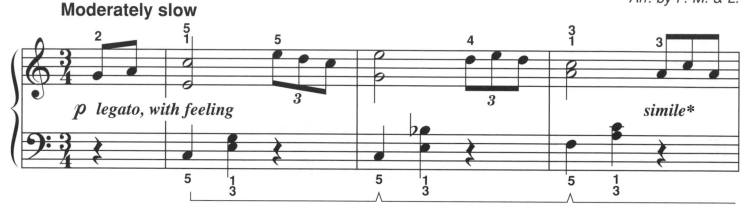

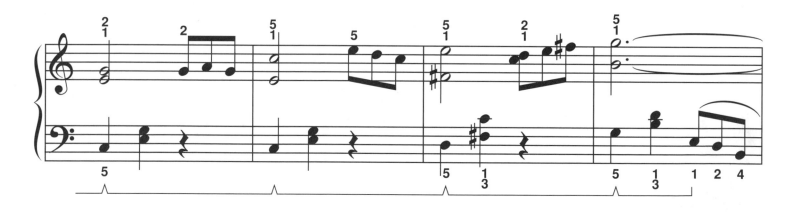

simile = same. This means *continue playing in the same manner.* In this case, continue to play triplets each time three eighth notes are joined with one beam.

On pages 96 to 111 are seven very popular selections that you have the knowledge and ability to perform.

OVER THE RAINBOW

Music by Harold Arlen
Lyrics by E.Y. Harburg

At Last

Music by Harry Warren
Lyrics by Mack Gordon

Slowly, with feeling

At last my love has come a - long,
last the skies a - bove are blue,

my lone - ly days are o - ver and life is like a
my heart was wrapped in clo - ver the night I looked at

1. song. At
you.

2. I found a

dream that I can speak to, a dream that I can call my

* The eighth notes may be played a bit unevenly: long short long short, *etc.*

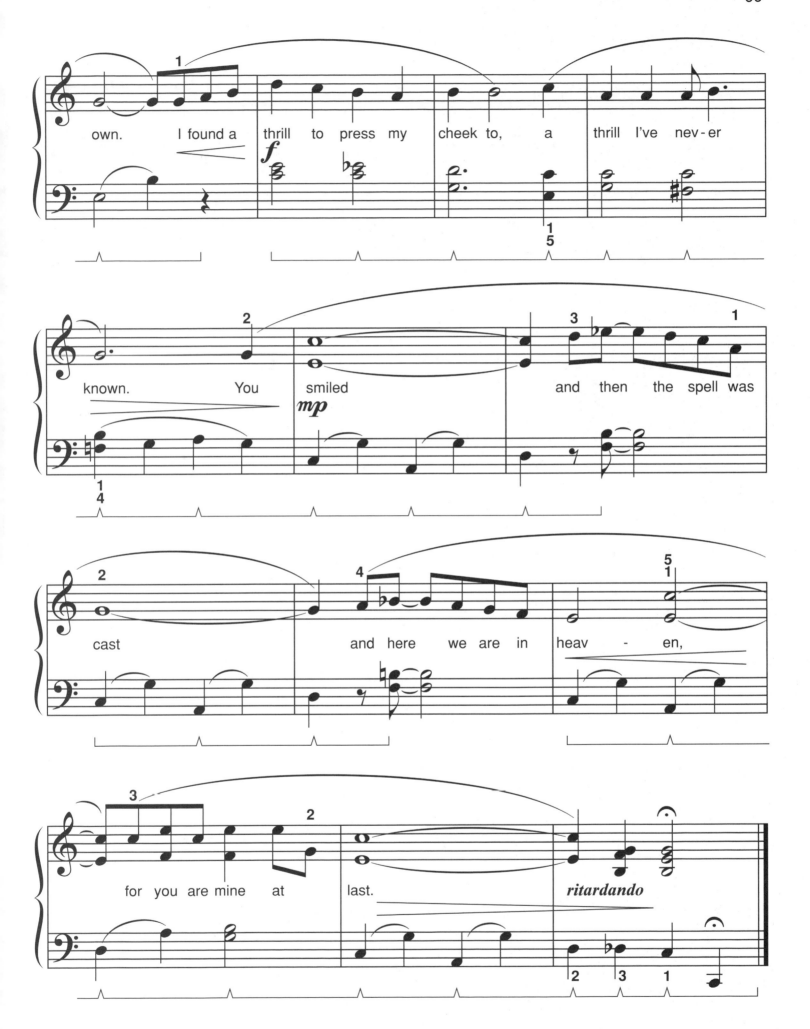

Singin' in the Rain

Music by Nacio Herb Brown
Lyric by Arthur Freed

* The eighth notes may be played a bit unevenly:

long short long short, *etc.*

LAURA

Lyrics by Johnny Mercer
Music by David Raksin

Slowly, with expression

Have Yourself a Merry Little Christmas

Words and Music by
Hugh Martin and Ralph Blane

Here we are as in old-en days, hap-py gold-en days of yore;

faith-ful friends who are dear to us gath-er near to us once more.

Through the years we all will be to-geth-er, if the Fates al - low.

Hang a shin-ing star up-on the high-est bough. And

have your-self a mer-ry lit-tle Christ-mas now.

THE BALLAD OF GILLIGAN'S ISLE

Words and Music by
Sherwood Schwartz and George Wyle

CHATTANOOGA CHOO CHOO

Music by Harry Warren
Lyrics by Mack Gordon

* A short note played quickly before the main note is called a *grace note.*

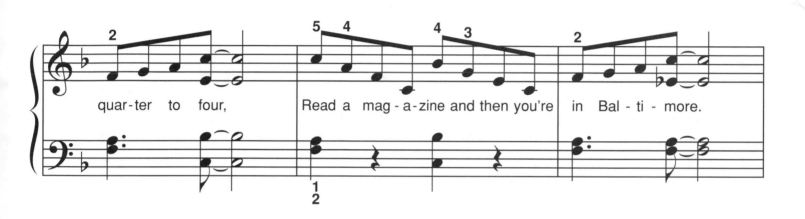

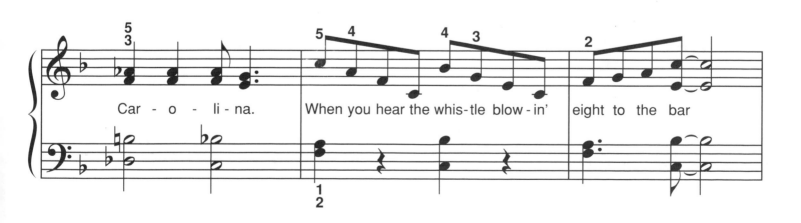

Then you know that Ten-nes-see is not ver - y far. Shov-el all the coal in,

got - ta keep it roll-in'. Woo, woo, Chat-ta-noo-ga, there you are.

There's gon-na be a cer-tain par - ty at the sta - tion,

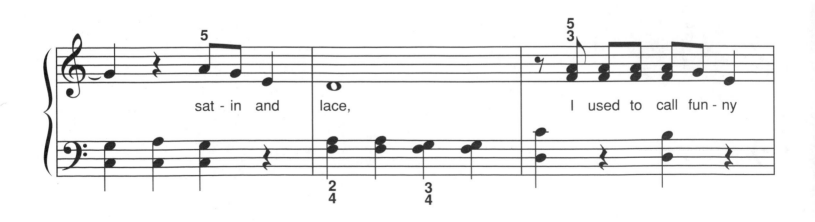

sat - in and lace, I used to call fun - ny